THE
HALF-PINT
GUIDE TO
CRAFT
BREWERIES

SOUTHERN CALIFORNIA

Nigel Quinney and Deirdre Greene

Roaring Forties Press
1053 Santa Fe Avenue
Berkeley, CA 94706
www.roaringfortiespress.com

Cover design by Kim Rusch; interior design by Nigel Quinney.

ISBN 978-1-938901-73-7 (print)
ISBN 978-1-938901-74-4 (ebook)

Contents

Introduction

Welcome to *The Half-Pint Guide!*

(That's pretty much it! We just wanted to say hello and welcome. If you want to skip the rest of this introduction, please go right ahead and do so. This is, after all, only a book. You've seen books before. You know how they work. No batteries, instructions, ID, or shirt and shoes required. This little book is full of some of the best craft breweries in Southern California, and if you want to know what their founders and brewers think about them, just dive right in. But if you're one of those people who like to know what they're getting themselves into, then, please, let us bend your ear for a couple of minutes.)

We wrote this book for people like us. People who enjoy chatting with a brewer across a bar about favorite beers, biggest achievements, and funniest stories. People who have stumbled on a fabulous brewery that they had no idea even existed. People who—scary thought!—have found themselves in an unfamiliar corner of California and realized, "OMG, I do not know where the nearest craft brewery is. Help!"

So, we thought we'd put together a guide that does three things.

One of those things is to cover great breweries in lots of different parts of the state, not just in the hoppy hot spots. The idea is that if you're from the mountains visiting the beach, or from the beach visiting the desert, or from . . . well, you get the idea, this book will help you find a fine place to wet your whistle.

The second thing is not only to provide nuts-and-bolts information about each brewery—important but basic stuff like where it is and when it's open—but also to dig deeper and uncover a brewery's story and personality. What makes it tick, what makes its founders proud, what do its regulars like best about it?

And the third thing is to let the breweries tell that story themselves, in their own words. As you'll see once you stop reading this introduction (if you haven't already!) and start dipping into the rest of the book, we asked each brewery more or less the same questions. The answers, though, are often wildly different—as different and as wild as the brewers and the breweries themselves.

A lot of books about beer are written by people who know a lot about beer and have a lot of opinions about breweries. And that is cool. But it's also sometimes a bit boring, because professional beer drinkers (now, there's a job!) and full-time critics can get a little jaded and carry around some big biases. One of the best things about visiting California's craft breweries is that wherever you go, you meet friendly brewers full of energy, enthusiasm, and passion for what they're doing—and for what their fellow brewers are doing on the next block or in the next town. This book is filled with that spirit. It's also filled with the kind of information and stories that only a brewer or an owner can tell you about his or her beer and brewery.

You might think that all that information and all those stories would easily fill a 1,000-barrel fermenter. Yet, here they are in a book called *The Half-Pint Guide*—a name inspired in large part by its small size. Why didn't we produce a book the size of the Beijing telephone directory?

The simple answer is that we wanted to end up with a book small enough to keep in your car's glove compartment or to fit in the back pocket of your jeans. (Try it! It really does fit in your back pocket—unless you're very petite or unless you're not so very petite but are wearing very petite jeans.) Keeping it half-pint sized also meant that we had to be selective, not comprehensive, in our coverage. So, we aimed to showcase around 100 breweries, spread out across the region, each one of them fabulous, innovative, or individual in its own way. Some well-known breweries are not included, and some are; some of the breweries in here have been around since before the craft beer revolution started, and some are new additions to the dynamically changing, still-expanding craft beer landscape.

As you already know, craft brewing in California is a certifiable phenomenon. From small beginnings thirty years ago, it has blossomed—no, not blossomed, it's exploded—into a force of nature, a volcano of creativity, a tsunami of flavors washing over a land where beer drinkers once had few (and, let's be honest, pretty boring) choices. A few years ago, you'd walk into a bar and be faced with the same question: "Bud or Miller?" Today, you walk into a craft brewery and have an alphabet of options: an altbier or an amber, a blonde or a brown, a chocolate stout or a cream ale . . . all the way through to wits, wild ales, and winter warmers.

And what and who do we have to thank for this amazing choice? Small-scale businesses created and run by people who prize individuality and inventiveness, who love the beers they brew, who relish the chance to experiment with new beers, and who want to give other people the chance to love them. (Oh, and we should also thank ourselves, we who love that chance. If it wasn't for our heroic, selfless readiness to drink an always wonderful, often wild, and sometimes downright weird assortment of delicious beers, where would those craft brewers be? Just saying . . .)

We mention this because (A) it's true, and (B) it helped us define what we mean by a "craft brewery." A craft brewery, in our eyes, is a brewery owned by itself, not by a big, faceless corporation that owns lots and lots of things, that is in business purely for the money, and that measures its pleasure in IPOs and LBOs, not in ABVs and IBUs. We know that some craft breweries are owned in part by other craft breweries, and we're OK with that. But if a small brewery is owned by big business, you're not likely to find it in this book—simply because, if big business continues to snaffle up small breweries, creativity and diversity will give way to conformity and profitability, and we'll all be back to the old days of "Bud or Miller?" (Not that there's anything wrong with those two fine pilsners, but who wants a beer alphabet with just two letters?)

Ok, we've taken enough of your time. Please go and explore the rest of the book, which we hope you'll find not only a handy guide but also an interesting and sometimes eye-opening read. But before you head off, let us just mention a few housekeeping matters:

• The opening hours (like the street addresses and phone numbers) were accurate when we did the research for this book, but please check on a brewery's website before you head out in case those hours have recently changed.

• We've arranged the book into seven different geographic regions of Southern California: San Diego (the city, plus areas south and east); North County, San Diego; Orange County; Los Angeles County; the Central Coast (the counties of Ventura, Santa Barbara, and San Luis Obispo); the Inland Empire (Riverside and Imperial Counties); and Imperial and Kern counties (which are at opposite ends of SoCal, where craft beer is harder to find and craft breweries are thus particularly welcome!). The map on page 1 shows how we've divided up Southern California. A few breweries have locations in more than one region. In this book, however, we do not feature the same brewery in more than one location.

• There's a list of abbreviations on the next page. So, if you're not sure what "ABV" or "IBU" stands for, take a look.

• There's an index near the end of the book listing all the breweries that are included in the book alphabetically, so if you want to know at a glance which breweries are here, and on what page, take a quick look at that.

• Right at the end of the book are some blank pages for you to jot down notes about the breweries you visit—or, if you prefer, you could use them to doodle pictures or play tic-tac-toe (a game invented, it's believed, by the ancient Egyptians, who really loved their beer).

• Please don't drink and drive. What are friends (or taxis) for?

Ok, we're done—there's nothing more to see here. But there's a state full of great beer to explore. And *The Half-Pint Guide* would love to tag along. ❄

Abbreviations

ABV: alcohol by volume—a measurement of how much alcohol is in a given volume of a beverage. The higher the ABV percentage, the stronger the beer.

BBL: barrels—the standard size for a barrel in the United States is 31 gallons. Brewhouses are classified by the siuze they produce. Many craft breweries brew in 7- or 10-barrel batches.

GABF: Great American Beer Festival—a huge and prestigious beer event that takes place in Denver every year.

IBU: International Bitterness Units—a measurement of how bitter a beer is. The higher the IBU number, the more bitter the beer.

Southern California

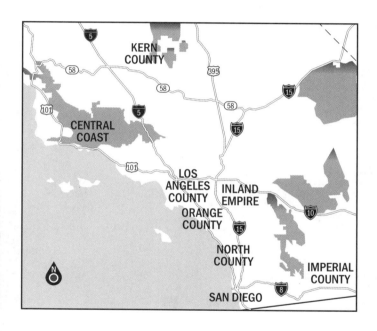

San Diego

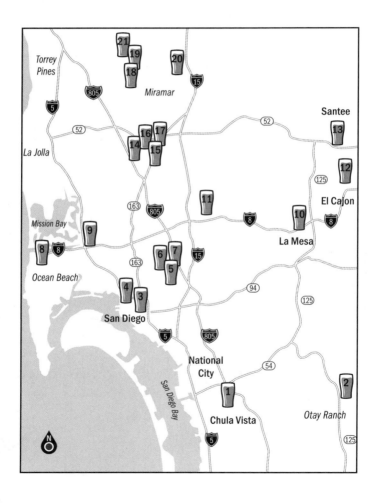

1. 3 Punk Ales, 259 Third Ave., Chula Vista
2. Novo Brazil Brewing, 901 Lane Ave., Chula Vista
3. Knotty Brewing Co., 842 Market St., San Diego
4. Bolt Brewery, 1971 India St., San Diego
5. North Park Beer Co., 3038 University Ave, San Diego
6. Home Brewing Co., 2911 El Cajon Blvd., San Diego
7. Eppig Brewing Co., 3052 El Cajon Blvd., San Diego
8. Ocean Beach Brewery, 5041 Newport Ave, San Diego
9. Deft Brewing, 5328 Banks St., San Diego
10. Helix Brewing Co., 8101 Commercial St., La Mesa
11. Benchmark Brewing Co., 6190 Fairmount Ave., San Diego
12. Burning Beard Brewing Co., 785 Vernon Way, El Cajon
13. Pacific Islander Brewing Co., 8665 Argent St., Santee
14. Circle 9 Brewing, 7292 Opportunity Rd., San Diego
15. Quantum Brewing, 5375 Kearny Villa Rd., San Diego
16. Societe Brewing Co., 8262 Clairemont Mesa Blvd., San Diego
17. Helm's Brewing Co., 5640 Kearny Mesa Rd., San Diego
18. 32 North Brewing Co., 8655 Production Ave., San Diego
19. Division 23 Brewing, 7408 Trade St., San Diego
20. Intergalactic Brewing Co., 9715 Carroll Centre Rd., San Diego
21. Longship Brewery, 10320 Camino Santa Fe, San Diego

3 PUNK ALES

259 Third Ave., Chula Vista, CA 91910
619-876-2513 • 3PunkAles.com

Mon.-Wed. noon-10 pm; Thurs. noon-11 pm;
Fri. & Sat. noon-midnight; Sun. 10 am-10 pm

WHEN DID YOU OPEN?
August 2017.

WHAT ARE YOUR MOST POPULAR BEERS?
La Flama Blanca (lager); Kill the Pour (IPA).

WHICH BEERS ARE YOU PROUDEST OF?
Needle in the Hey! First beer we ever brewed as Thr3e Punk Ales . . . four years ago.

HAVE YOUR BEERS WON ANY AWARDS?
We have yet to enroll our brews in any contests. Soon.

WHAT ARE THE BIGGEST CHALLENGES YOUR BREWERY HAS FACED?
Our biggest challenge was actually getting open. We faced every possible obstacle prior to opening up shop. But, alas . . . we're finally open. Oh, and our beertender Bruno, he's definitely challenged.

WHAT'S THE ATMOSPHERE LIKE?
We put beer, punk music, and soccer into a blender and out came Thr3e Punk.

ARE YOU DOG & FAMILY FRIENDLY?
Both, yes.

DO YOU HAVE FOOD?
Food trucks only.

WHAT ELSE CAN YOU TELL US?
Our brewery may be haunted . . . for realzzz.

We love soccer, and we show all the matches at our tasting room . . . we are privy to Manchester United.

We have an employee by the name of Albert "Small Teeth" Aguirre, who has the tiniest, cutest teeth you could imagine. ❄

2

NOVO BRAZIL

901 Lane Ave., Chula Vista, CA 91914
619-869-4274 • novobrazilbrewing.com

Sun.-Thurs. noon-10 pm;
Fri. & Sat. noon-midnight

WHEN DID YOU OPEN?
April 2015.

WHAT ARE YOUR MOST POPULAR BEERS?
Bossa Haze, The Mango IPA, Ipanema DIPA, Chula Pils, and Corvo Negro Imperial Stout.

WHICH BEERS ARE YOU PROUDEST OF?
Bossa—all malt and huge hop bill. Corvo—bronze at World Beer cup. The Mango because it is so versatile.

HAVE YOUR BEERS WON ANY AWARDS?
Many awards, but no GABF yet. Best of San Diego, 2016, *San Diego Magazine*; *City Beat Magazine*, Top 5 New Breweries in San Diego; 2016 bronze medal, SD International Beer Fest.

WHAT ARE THE BIGGEST CHALLENGES YOUR BREWERY HAS FACED?
Growing pains in the brewhouse.

WHAT'S THE ATMOSPHERE LIKE?
Beautiful, fun, worth the drive.

ARE YOU DOG & FAMILY FRIENDLY?
Yes and yes.

Do you have food?

Food trucks on most days. Check the website.

What else can you tell us?

We are about great beer in a fun environment, and we march to the (Brazilian) beat of our own drum. ❁

3

KNOTTY BREWING CO.

842 Market St., San Diego, CA 92101
619-269-4337 • knottybrewing.com

Mon.–Thurs. 5–9 pm; Fri. 5–11 pm;
Sat. noon–11 pm; Sun. noon–8 pm

WHEN DID YOU OPEN?

2016.

WHAT ARE YOUR MOST POPULAR BEERS?

Tom Tom Blonde Super Fresh Pale Ale; Kasie's Stout Clay IPA.

WHICH BEERS ARE YOU PROUDEST OF?

Our blonde has a light, crisp drinkability, made with organic grapefruit, and its own unique style. Our stout is a big, delicious, robust stout, but it is very drinkable and refreshing, which is not often seen in this style.

HAVE YOUR BEERS WON ANY AWARDS?

Not yet, but we are sure they will.

WHAT ARE THE BIGGEST CHALLENGES YOUR BREWERY HAS FACED?

Having enough space and time, just like any other brewery, we're sure.

WHAT'S THE ATMOSPHERE LIKE?

We are a very small neighborhood brewery with a small tasting room and the smallest patio in East Village San Diego. Most of our customers love our tasting room because it is very chill.

DO YOU HAVE FOOD?

We do not, but we are attached to our brew-pub, and customers can order food from there.

WHAT ELSE CAN YOU TELL US?

Most of our beers are named after regular customers or people who have had some influence on our business. We loaded all our brewing equipment into our tiny brewery with the help of six people and a broken dolly. ✻

4

BOLT BREWERY

1971 India St., San Diego, CA 92101
619-795-3012 • boltbrewery.com

Sun.–Tues. 11 am–10 pm; Wed. & Thurs. 11 am–11 pm;
Fri. & Sat. 11–1 am

8179 Center St., La Mesa, CA 91942
619-303-7837 • boltbrewery.com

Mon.–Wed. 1–9 pm; Thurs. 1–10 pm;
Fri. & Sat. 11 am–11 pm; Sun. 11 am–9 pm

WHEN DID YOU OPEN?

December 2014.

WHAT ARE YOUR MOST POPULAR BEERS?

OG IPA; Mango Me Crazy Ale.

WHICH BEERS ARE YOU PROUDEST OF?

We are proud of all of our beers—we brew to impress.

HAVE YOUR BEERS WON ANY AWARDS?

Not yet.

WHAT ARE THE BIGGEST CHALLENGES YOUR BREWERY HAS FACED?

Meeting the demand for our delicious beers!

WHAT'S THE ATMOSPHERE LIKE?

In San Diego, we keep it casual; we strive to make it a place to relax and enjoy. Our outdoor beer garden in La Mesa has been described as a hidden jewel. Being all outdoors really gives you the relaxed backyard feel. With barbecues for customers to use and picnic tables, it's somewhere you can hang out all day and feel right at home.

ARE YOU DOG & FAMILY FRIENDLY?

Family friendly, dog friendly on the patio (San Diego); adult only after 7 pm Fri. and Sat. (La Mesa).

DO YOU HAVE FOOD?

Yes: burgers, sandwiches, and salads (San Diego); occasional food trucks but no kitchen (La Mesa).

WHAT ELSE CAN YOU TELL US?

Bolt Brewery was originally started in 1987 and was the first commercial brewery in San Diego County. Clint Stromberg was one of the original brewers at Bolt, as well as the youngest commercial brewer in the United States from 1987 to 1990. Today, Clint is the brewmaster for Bolt, and he continues to brew amazing beer. ❈

NORTH PARK BEER CO.

3038 University Ave., San Diego, CA 92104
(619) 255-2946 • northpark.beer

Mon.-Thurs. 3-10 pm; Fri. noon-midnight;
Sat. 10 am-midnight; Sun. 9-10 am yoga, 10 am-midnight

WHEN DID YOU OPEN?

June 2016.

WHAT ARE YOUR MOST POPULAR BEERS?

Hop-Fu!, our West Coast IPA; Covington, our classic American cream ale; Golden Phoenix, our golden oatmeal milk stout served on nitro; Art Is Hard, our New England-style IPA.

WHICH BEERS ARE YOU PROUDEST OF?

Once brewed in our founder's home garage, Hop-Fu! IPA was the single most award-winning homebrewed IPA in the entire world! It is now the flagship beer at our brewery.

HAVE YOUR BEERS WON ANY AWARDS?

Founder Kelsey McNair won many awards as a homebrewer prior to opening North Park Beer Co. Since opening the brewery, our Covington Cream Ale and Bird Park Bohemian Pilsner have won awards in commercial beer competitions. The readers of local beer publication *West Coaster* named our Hop-Fu! IPA the best San Diego IPA in the best 16 of '16 poll.

WHAT ARE THE BIGGEST CHALLENGES YOUR BREWERY HAS FACED?

We had a number of construction-related issues that caused major delays in opening. It is good to be past that stage and operating a popular brewery and taproom.

WHAT'S THE ATMOSPHERE LIKE?

Our taproom is a warm, welcoming, neighborhood gathering place that is clad with high-end finishes such as copper, quarter-sawn white oak, and blackened steel.

Are you dog & family friendly?

We are a 100 percent family-friendly brewery. Due to our on-site kitchen, we're not allowed to have dogs in the taproom. However, we're planning to add a dog-friendly patio in the near future.

Do you have food?

Our brewery has a kitchen operated by popular food truck and catering company Mastiff Sausage Company. Mastiff serves casual beer-friendly pub fare. Try the Mastiff fries or pork nugs!

What else can you tell us?

We have a mezzanine-level events space that can be booked for private parties and accommodates more than 80 guests.

We offer free yoga every Sunday at 9 am.

We have a Beer Brunch every Saturday and Sunday from 10 am to 3 pm that includes beer cocktails. ❂

6

HOME BREWING CO.

2911 El Cajon Blvd., San Diego, CA 92104
619-450-6165 • homebrewingco.com

Mon. 11 am–6 pm; Tues. & Wed. 11 am–8 pm; Thurs. & Fri. 11 am–10 pm;
Sat. 10 am–10 pm; Sun. 10 am–6 pm

WHEN DID YOU OPEN?

2015.

WHAT ARE YOUR MOST POPULAR BEERS?

go-[zuh] our light, traditional-style gose; Sharks with Lasers, a fruity/resinous West Coast IPA; Commoditization of Hype, an infinitely crushable American lager.

WHICH BEERS ARE YOU PROUDEST OF?

All of them! We take a lot of time to research the style, ingredients, history, and process. We're all students of beer, so each beer receives just as much attention and commitment to high standards as the last.

HAVE YOUR BEERS WON ANY AWARDS?

Not yet. Our team includes experienced beer judges, so we are constantly judging our own beers, but competitions have not been our primary focus.

WHAT ARE THE BIGGEST CHALLENGES YOUR BREWERY HAS FACED?

Letting people know that we're not just a homebrew supply store that happens to have a brewery. We take our brewery and our store seriously, and we want every customer to feel like they are getting the best experience of either.

WHAT'S THE ATMOSPHERE LIKE?

Laid-back, yet attentive and always friendly.

ARE YOU DOG & FAMILY FRIENDLY?

Yes, we appreciate every member of the family.

DO YOU HAVE FOOD?

Not yet; we're working on connecting with our neighbors to install a service window for food and a menu that will feature local chefs.

H⌂ME
BREWING CO.

WHAT ELSE CAN YOU TELL US?

We are beer geeks who take the beer seriously, but not ourselves. Our favorite event is "Trashy Hour": the third Sunday of the month, noon to 2 pm, we pro-vide trash bags, gloves, etc. We all go around the neighborhood for 30 minutes to collect trash, then come back for $3 pints. ✳

7

EPPIG BREWING CO.

3052 El Cajon Blvd., Ste. C, San Diego, CA 92104
619-501-1840 • eppigbrewing.com

Mon.-Thurs. 4-9 pm; Fri. 3-10 pm;
Sat. noon-10 pm; Sun. noon-9 pm

WHEN DID YOU OPEN?
October 2016.

WHAT ARE YOUR MOST POPULAR BEERS?
10:45 to Denver IPA; Civility San Diego Summer Ale; Natural Bridge Lager Series.

WHICH BEERS ARE YOU PROUDEST OF?
Natural Bridge—Festbier. It is a very traditional take on a German-style lager that translates perfectly for enjoying the Southern California weather.

HAVE YOUR BEERS WON ANY AWARDS?
In 2017, at the San Diego International Beer Festival, our IWCBD Kottbusser won gold, our Glitz and Glam won silver, and our Natural Bridge—Baltic Porter and Sinister Path won bronzes; at the LA International Beer Festival, IWCBD Kottbusser won a gold medal and Natural Bridge—Schwarzbier won a silver; and at the Cal. State Fair, our Natural Bridge-Schwarzbier and our Natural Bridge-Zwickelbier won silver medals.

WHAT ARE THE BIGGEST CHALLENGES YOUR BREWERY HAS FACED?
Keeping up with demand while being constrained by our brewery size.

WHAT'S THE ATMOSPHERE LIKE?
Warm and inviting, family friendly, fucking awesome.

DO YOU HAVE FOOD?
No.

WHAT ELSE CAN YOU TELL US?
Established 1866, reinvented 2016: Eppig Brewing was resurrected in 2016 by Stephanie Eppig and her partners, 150 years after the Eppig family's

first brewery was established in Brooklyn, NY. Our Natural Bridge Lager Series tells the story of the original founders of Eppig Brewing traveling from Germany to Brooklyn, establishing roots and lager brewing traditions. We have chosen to continue on that path in San Diego, brewing a broad range of styles, drawing from the rich family brewing tradition while innovating to create beers that are distinctly our own.

Our brewhouse location is a former gentleman's club, and two of our beers are named after the building's former glory. ❊

OCEAN BEACH BREWERY

5041 Newport Ave., San Diego CA 92107
619-955-8053 • obbrewingco.com

Mon.-Thurs. 11 am–10 pm; Fri. 11 am–11 pm;
Sat. 10 am–11 pm; Sun. 10 am–9 pm

WHEN DID YOU OPEN?
July 2016.

WHAT ARE YOUR MOST POPULAR BEERS?
The Hidden Gem Dunkelweizen and our Long Time Comin' Cream Ale.

WHICH BEERS ARE YOU PROUDEST OF?
The dunkelweizen. Because it was our first silver medal winner at the GABF.

HAVE YOUR BEERS WON ANY AWARDS?
Silver, GABF 2017.

WHAT ARE THE BIGGEST CHALLENGES YOUR BREWERY HAS FACED?

Being a three-level brewery with seating on all three levels. Maintenance on a building that big is a bit of a challenge.

WHAT'S THE ATMOSPHERE LIKE?

We have a very relaxed vibe. We are the epitome of Ocean Beach, with a great mix of chill tunes, a laid-back atmosphere, and a great place to watch the sunset with a good sandwich and a cold brew.

ARE YOU DOG & FAMILY FRIENDLY?

Yes on both. Kids' menu as well.

DO YOU HAVE FOOD?

Yes. We have upscale pub fare. Fish n' chips, burgers and fries, shrimp and cheddar grits, chicken sandwiches, pita tacos with fish, carnitas, or chicken. House-made garlicky hummus and pita, blue crab guacamole with chips. We also have a simple brunch menu including two different types of Benedicts and omelets, a breakfast quesadilla, and salmon salsa grits and eggs.

WHAT ELSE CAN YOU TELL US?

We are the only three-story restaurant in OB. The building used to be a police station as well as a Planned Parenthood office before it became a brewery. ✳

9

DEFT BREWING

5328 Banks St., San Diego, CA 92110
858-999-5728 • deftbrewing.com

Mon.-Thurs. 4-8 pm; Fri. noon-10 pm;
Sat. 11 am-10 pm; Sun. 11 am-8 pm

WHEN DID YOU OPEN?

October 2017.

WHAT ARE YOUR MOST POPULAR BEERS?

DeftHopt Golden English IPA, Rhein Sonnenschein Kolsch-Style Ale, Golden Mule Light Golden Ale with Lime and Ginger.

WHICH BEERS ARE YOU PROUDEST OF?

Frankly, we are proud of our entire menu, which does veer a bit from the hoppier path taken by most San Diego breweries. Our West European styles—including German, Belgian, British, and Irish ales—have been welcomed by the San Diego beer-drinking community as a refreshing change of pace. A great example is the Dusseldeft Secret, a "sticke" style altbier. This rare style is a nice mix of prominent malt presence, enough underlying hop character for balance, and with more ABV strength than in the base style. Of the hoppier offerings, we are proud of our DeftHopt Golden, which is brewed in the tradition of a classic English IPA with significant malt influence, yet this one is dry-hopped with a great combination of familiar American hops to make for a flavorful yet balanced IPA experience.

HAVE YOUR BEERS WON ANY AWARDS?

Some of our beer recipes—or their predecessors—won awards from their homebrew competitions, but we have not yet entered our beers into commercial competitions.

WHAT ARE THE BIGGEST CHALLENGES YOUR BREWERY HAS FACED?

Time. During construction, when we were slogging through the licensing and permitting phases, everything seemed to move so slowly. Now that we have opened and are in the full swing of things, we are at hyper speed and there are not enough hours in the day to get everything done. For this reason, we have yet to launch a robust marketing effort to get the word out about Deft Brewing. Until we do, we have to rely on word of mouth and more organic growth.

WHAT'S THE ATMOSPHERE LIKE?

Our brewery space is more often described by our guests as "cool," "comfortable," and "airy." The building is an old fishing boat manufacturing building, with a history so fitting for San Diego.

ARE YOU DOG & FAMILY FRIENDLY?

Deft Brewing is very much dog and kid friendly. As our tasting room poster notes, we love and welcome behaved dogs on a leash. In the tasting room, we provide a large dog bowl and free treats for the pooches. As for kids, Deft Brewing provides a fun little "Deft Kids" zone with a small puppet show theater and puppets, chalkboard, toys, and games.

DO YOU HAVE FOOD?

Although we do not serve food at Deft Brewing, we have a stable of five well-known, high-quality food trucks on our schedule. We also have numerous great restaurants within three or four blocks of Deft and many others that deliver.

WHAT ELSE CAN YOU TELL US?

Deft is an adjective often used to describe artists that means "to demonstrate skill or cleverness." Both of us who founded Deft are mechanical engineers. Engineers are hired to solve problems and become quite good at it, but we take extra pride in being able to solve problems in a deft sort of way. Deft is how we want our guests to think about us and our beer—that we demonstrated great skill and cleverness in making our creations.

My wife and I are longtime Bay Park residents with a home a couple miles from the brewery. We know and love this community and, through our research, we realized that it could support a brewery and tasting room like ours, despite the otherwise crowded market in San Diego.

Our patio includes a live hop garden where we grow Cascade, Chinook, and Centennial hops. Over the spring and summer, those hop bines grow up the patio fence, then create a canopy over the outdoor patio seating area, making it a fun and enjoyable space to sample our beers. In fact, the hops we harvested from those bines last year were actually used in the first batch of our DeftHopt Golden English IPA, and we plan to do the same this fall. It doesn't get much more locally grown than that! �֍

HELIX BREWING CO.

8101 Commercial St., La Mesa, CA 91942
619-741-8447 • drinkhelix.com

Mon.–Thurs. 3–9 pm; Fri. & Sat. noon–10 pm;
Sun. noon–7 pm

WHEN DID YOU OPEN?
August 2015.

WHAT ARE YOUR MOST POPULAR BEERS?
Helix Pale Ale, Active IPA, Galaxy Rye IPA, and Stoner Moment. All are great examples of style and push the limit of craft beer.

HAVE YOUR BEERS WON ANY AWARDS?
We haven't entered any yet.

WHAT'S THE ATMOSPHERE LIKE?
Homey, unique, old red brick, open; all brewing equipment and process visible, no wall except in the restroom; outdoor beer patio with giant tree.

ARE YOU DOG & FAMILY FRIENDLY?
Kid friendly, dog friendly, grandparents friendly.

WHAT ELSE CAN YOU TELL US?
Started by a local homebrewer in La Mesa who grew up in La Mesa. An engineer who turned to beer.

We also brew sour beer. ❊

BENCHMARK BREWING CO.

6190 Fairmount Ave., Suite G, San Diego, CA 92120
4112 Napier St., San Diego, CA 92110
619-795-2911 • benchmarkbrewing.com

We are open seven days a week;
hours of operation vary by season and location

WHEN DID YOU OPEN?

2013.

WHAT ARE YOUR MOST POPULAR BEERS?

By the numbers, IPA (our Core Session IPA); by request, Beaten Path XPA, Survey Series IPAs (both have limited availability).

WHICH BEERS ARE YOU PROUDEST OF?

Table Beer and Oatmeal Stout. Table Beer is a bright, refreshing flavorful beer. Oatmeal Stout often surprises people: it is flavorful with the body of a higher-ABV beer.

HAVE YOUR BEERS WON ANY AWARDS?

Oatmeal Stout took gold in 2014 and silver in 2016 at GABF in the session beer category; Table Beer has a silver award from the 2014 SD International Beer Competition (SDIBC); Blond Ale has a bronze from the 2015 SDIBC; Voyager, our Belgian-style dubbel, has a bronze award from the 2016 SDIBC.

WHAT ARE THE BIGGEST CHALLENGES YOUR BREWERY HAS FACED?

Obtaining enough funding to support growth.

WHAT'S THE ATMOSPHERE LIKE?

We are a neighborhood spot. The decor is inviting and comfortable, but clean. We aim to be the

BEER FLAVORED BEER

BENCHMARK BREWING COMPANY

"third place" (home and work being first and second) that every neighborhood needs, a place to run into your neighbors and enjoy a chat over a beer. We aim to be approachable and knowledgeable about our product and beer in general. Our beer reflects this ethos: we have something for everyone; beer that is approachable but refined; and, although our core beers focus on lower ABV styles, we offer a wide range of flavors and alcohol levels through our Parks Collection (special releases) and High Ground series (seasonal releases).

ARE YOU DOG & FAMILY FRIENDLY?

Yes, kids and dogs are welcome; we expect both to be well supervised/leashed as appropriate.

DO YOU HAVE FOOD?

Nope, just beer . . . beer-flavored beer to be exact. We welcome customers to bring in a meal, order a pizza, or enjoy one of our packaged snacks from the bar. We do host food trucks oc-

casionally, but generally only for special events.

WHAT ELSE CAN YOU TELL US?

Our master brewer and cofounder Matt Akin was at AleSmith for more than eight years, starting at keg scrubber and working up to head brewer in about three years.

We make what we call beer-flavored beer: we use traditional ingredients to bring the flavor in our beers—no coffee or grapefruit here.

Our HQ is located on the banks of the San Diego River; we work closely with the San Diego River Park Foundation to clean up and reclaim the waterway. We hope one day to relocate our tasting room to the end of the building and open up the fencing for a riverfront tasting room.

Benchmark has an actual USGS-style benchmark set into a large rock inside the tasting room. ❄

25

BURNING BEARD BREWING CO.

785 Vernon Way, El Cajon, CA 92020
619-456-9185 • burningbeardbrewing.com

Mon.–Wed. noon–9 pm; Thurs.–Sat. noon–10 pm;
Sun. noon–7 pm

WHEN DID YOU OPEN?
April 2016.

WHAT ARE YOUR MOST POPULAR BEERS?
Hopmata, a West Coast IPA; Strung Out on Lasers, a San Diego unfiltered IPA; Circle of Hops, a pale ale; Normcore, a Czech pils; ESB; Banksy.

WHICH BEERS ARE YOU PROUDEST OF?
Normcore. We are very proud of this because this style is like running naked through the brewhouse. It is light and subtle and there is nowhere for imperfections to hide. Our reputation is on full display with this beer.

HAVE YOUR BEERS WON ANY AWARDS?

Yes, Cal. State Fair gold for our ESB, Banksy; Cal. State Fair silver for our trappiest single, Get Thee to a Nunnery; Cal. State Fair bronze for our pale ale, Circle of Hops.

We took the *West Coaster* Beer of the Year in 2016 with our Czech pils, Normcore.

WHAT ARE THE BIGGEST CHALLENGES YOUR BREWERY HAS FACED?

Personal OCD at all levels, with all employees. We all care a lot.

WHAT'S THE ATMOSPHERE LIKE?

Our brewery has a killer vibe. We tried to transcend the typical brewery/tasting room feel and inject our own personality into the space.

Phrases customers have used to describe the brewery: "It is like a rock n' roll Valhalla."

ARE YOU DOG & FAMILY FRIENDLY?

Yes.

DO YOU HAVE FOOD?

We truck it in.

WHAT ELSE CAN YOU TELL US?

Cofounders Jeff and Mike were old snowboarding friends.

Both Jeff and Mike have advanced literature degrees and incorporate their love of literature, music, and art into their beer names: see if you can discover each beer name origin. They also curated a jukebox in the taproom that customers flip over.

Our tasting room manager, Shannon, is a direct descendant of the Norse God Freya.

We have twice as many female as male employees.

We took the 2016 *West Coaster* award for Brewery of the Year in San Diego. ✳

PACIFIC ISLANDER BEER CO.

8665 Argent St., Santee, CA 92071
619-270-7777 • pibbeer.com

Mon.-Thurs. 4–8 pm; Fri. 3–10 pm;
Sat. 1–10 pm; Sun. 1–7 pm

WHEN DID YOU OPEN?

2014.

WHAT ARE YOUR MOST POPULAR BEERS?

Li'ke Li'ke Honey Blonde Ale, Da'kine IPA, and Sunset Red Ale.

WHICH BEERS ARE YOU PROUDEST OF?

All of our beers. Our Honey Blonde is the highest-volume sales beer. It is a crisp, clean ale with a perfect splash of honey. Light bodied but still full of flavor, this is a great beer to introduce you to PIB craft beers. Mo'bettah DIPA is our craft beer with the taste of why we are in the brewery business. Why PIB Mo'bettah? Well, because it is Mo'bettah! This is a big, bold DIPA (double/imperial IPA) with a perfect mix of hops. Mo'bettah has a big smell, big body, and big flavor. This beer is what you would expect from a DIPA. Dry-hopped in two stages, this is a beer for the craft beer fan who loves hops and all the great flavors that they want

What's the atmosphere like?

Islander vibe. A family-run and -supported brewery. Sharing the aloha spirit with our customers.

Are you dog & family friendly?

We are kid and dog (on a leash) friendly.

Do you have food?

Food trucks Thursday through Sunday with awesome creations. You can bring food to the brewery anytime while enjoying our beers.

What else can you tell us?

Pacific Islander Beer Company is about Pacific Islands people. PIB brings back the memory of palm trees, a cool breeze, cold beers, and a vibe that only comes from our Islander experience. Islander music playing on the beautiful patio. Live Hawaiian music every Friday and Saturday, sporting events on TV, and a gaming area. There are also free event areas for private parties.

"Pacific Islander" is a geographic term to describe the inhabitants of any of the three major subregions of Oceania: Micronesia, Melanesia, and Polynesia. Head brewer Will Fox and cofounder Ku'uipo Lawler, both born with the aloha spirit, named the brewery after our heritage. ✳

in a craft beer. Mo'bettah means that we strive to do what is right in all that we do.

Have any of your beers won awards?

Five.

What are the biggest challenges your brewery has faced?

Growth. Distribution and being able to supply the demand. Larger breweries that have the financial strength to put more taps/brands in retail locations. Taxation and fees on being in business in California.

14

CIRCLE 9 BREWING

7292 Opportunity Rd., Suite C, San Diego, CA 92111
858-634-ALES • circle9brewing.com

Tue. & Wed. 3–9 pm; Thurs. 3–10 pm;
Fri. & Sat. noon–10 pm; Sun. 6–10 pm

WHEN DID YOU OPEN?
August 2017.

WHAT ARE YOUR MOST POPULAR BEERS?
City of Dis IPA.

WHICH OF YOUR BEERS ARE YOU PROUDEST OF?
City of Dis because after working on it for years we finally hit a new level, and Limbo Lager because of its unique ingredients—German yeast and Japanese rice—which give it a far more exciting flavor than most boring lagers.

WHAT ARE THE BIGGEST CHALLENGES YOUR BREWERY HAS FACED?
Keeping up with demand.

WHAT'S THE ATMOSPHERE LIKE?
Relaxed, unique.

ARE YOU DOG & FAMILY FRIENDLY?
Yes and yes.

DO YOU HAVE FOOD?
Food trucks and caterers.

WHAT ELSE CAN YOU TELL US?
The name Circle 9 refers to a level of hell in Dante's *Inferno*, which also provides the theme around which beers are named and listed (in the order of their ABV) on the brewery's menu board. ❄

QUANTUM BREWING

5375 Kearny Villa Rd., #116, San Diego, CA 92123
858-254-6481 • quantumbrewingsd.com

Mon.-Thurs. noon-8 pm; Fri. & Sat. noon-10 pm;
Sun. noon-6 pm

WHEN DID YOU OPEN?
July 2014.

WHAT ARE YOUR MOST POPULAR BEERS?
A blood orange wheat ale called Solar Flare; a blueberry cream ale called Cyano Cream Ale; a blonde ale called SD Summer Solstice; and an Irish red ale called 650 Nanometers.

WHICH BEERS ARE YOU PROUDEST OF?
650 Nanometers, because it's a perfectly balanced beer, full of flavors, and not too bitter.

WHAT'S THE ATMOSPHERE LIKE?
Welcoming and cozy.

ARE YOU DOG & FAMILY FRIENDLY?
Dog and family friendly.

DO YOU HAVE FOOD?
No, but we have the menus from all five restaurants in the strip mall. They deliver Italian, fine burgers, Mexican, Vietnamese, and Chinese.

WHAT ELSE CAN YOU TELL US?
We have trivia nights, cask nights, and two large-screen TVs. ✻

SOCIETE BREWING CO.

8262 Clairemont Mesa Blvd., San Diego, CA 92111
858-598-5409 • societebrewing.com

Mon.-Wed. noon-9 pm; Thurs.-Sat. noon-10 pm;
Sun. noon-8 pm (noon-9 pm in the summer)

WHEN DID YOU OPEN?
2012.

WHAT ARE YOUR MOST POPULAR BEERS?
The Pupil IPA, The Apprentice IPA, The Coachman Really Small IPA, The Harlot Belgian Extra, The Heiress Czech Pilsner, The Butcher Imperial Stout, The Swindler Feral Ale.

WHICH BEERS ARE YOU PROUDEST OF?
We are equally proud of all of our beers, but we are exceptionally proud of The Harlot Belgian Extra, a seemingly simple, 5.6 percent ABV beer that takes inspiration from Belgian-style ales and Czech pilsners, incorporating ingredients found in both to create a crisp, highly drinkable beer with myriad layers of flavor brought about by our house Belgian yeast strain.

HAVE YOUR BEERS WON ANY AWARDS?
Yes. The Coachman Really Small IPA won gold at the 2015 GABF; The Pugilist Dry Stout won silver at the 2014 World Beer Cup Classic; The Pupil IPA won bronze at the 2014 GABF; and The Volcanist American

Stout won bronze at the 2016 GABF.

WHAT ARE THE BIGGEST CHALLENGES YOUR BREWERY HAS FACED?

Supplying enough beer to the accounts that we would like to carry without expanding too fast.

WHAT'S THE ATMOSPHERE LIKE?

We love that many describe our brewery and tasting room as a "must-visit" location and that those in our local brewing industry describe it as "where the brewers drink when they're not brewing." We strive to offer a very open, welcoming environment centered around a turn-of-the-century thematic that is a rustic homage to creation, innovation, and ingenuity.

ARE YOU DOG & FAMILY FRIENDLY?

Family and dog friendly.

DO YOU HAVE FOOD?

We do not serve food, but we have mobile food vendors on site Tuesday through Sunday every week.

WHAT ELSE CAN YOU TELL US?

We bottle only our Feral ales (barrel-aged and wild beers); all of our other beers are draft only in our tasting room and beyond.

Our beers are split into four categories: (1) Out West: West Coast-style hoppy beers (IPAs, pale ales); (2) Old World: continental ales and lagers hailing from Belgium, Germany, and the Czech Republic (abbey ales, witbier, pilsner, Oktoberfest); (3) Stygian: dark ales (brown ales, stouts); and (4) Feral: barrel-aged and wild ales.

Our cofounding brewmaster, Travis Smith, was Russian River Brewing's original pub brewer, a position he held for five years before moving to The Bruery, where he met and brewed with our other cofounder, Douglas Constantiner, and conceived the idea they would later forge into reality: Societe Brewing Company. ✻

HELM'S BREWING CO.

5640 Kearny Mesa Rd., Unit C/N, San Diego, CA 92111
858-201-3097 • helmsbrewingco.com

Tasting room: 4896 Newport Ave., San Diego, CA 92107
619-795-1991 • helmsbrewingco.com

Hours are seasonal; check the website

WHEN DID YOU OPEN?
On a dark and stormy day in 2012.

WHAT ARE YOUR MOST POPULAR BEERS?
Imperial Walker IPA, Captain's Pale Ale, and our Citrus Radler.

WHICH BEERS ARE YOU PROUDEST OF?
We are very proud of our Beer-uccino coffee porter; it is our most recognized and awarded beer and uses locally roasted coffee beans.

HAVE YOUR BEERS WON ANY AWARDS?
Beeruccino.

WHAT ARE THE BIGGEST CHALLENGES YOUR BREWERY HAS FACED?
Market pressure! More than 150 breweries in SD!!

What's the atmosphere like?

Casual, coastal, welcoming vibe. Lots of locals, lots of new visitors. We are located on a busy street in one of America's last real beach towns.

Our favorite phrases: "We have an open-door policy; don't come in if our doors aren't open"; "Come in and drop anchor"; "Loose lips sink ships"; "We're anchored in San Diego."

Are you dog & family friendly?

Dogs, children, and outside food are welcome and encouraged. We offer a 20 percent doggie discount on Wednesdays. #houndsofhelms

Do you have food?

We do not, but we absolutely encourage bringing in a burrito or a sandwich from close by or from the Ocean Beach Farmers Market on Wednesdays.

What else can you tell us?

We are founded by shipbuilders, hence the name Helm's.

President Obama has a Helm's Brewery tattoo.

We use local ingredients, including hops, from our Ocean Beach community garden. ❖

32 NORTH BREWING CO.

8655 Production Ave., Suite A, San Diego, CA 92121
619-363-2622 • 32northbrew.com

Mon.-Thurs. 4–10 pm; Fri. & Sat. noon–10 pm;
Sun. noon–8 pm

WHEN DID YOU OPEN?

October 2014.

WHAT ARE YOUR MOST POPULAR BEERS?

Our Landfall Berliner Weisse has a following; our Best Coast IPA and Conqueror Pilsner are famous in San Diego for their quality.

WHICH BEERS ARE YOU PROUDEST OF?

We have had so many unique beers throughout the years that have been different from the status quo, it's tough to single out a few. Our BBA Russian Imperial Stout is going to be a great beer.

HAVE YOUR BEERS WON ANY AWARDS?

A few regional awards.

WHAT ARE THE BIGGEST CHALLENGES YOUR BREWERY HAS FACED?

Stiff competition and standing above the crowd.

WHAT'S THE ATMOSPHERE LIKE?

We have an industrial/rustic atmosphere that really resonates with people. It's a good space to play games or socialize in, so people typically describe it as "cool," "beautiful," and "chill."

ARE YOU DOG & FAMILY FRIENDLY?

Dog and kid friendly!

DO YOU HAVE FOOD?

We do not.

WHAT ELSE CAN YOU TELL US?

Most of our decor and furniture is handmade. Our name comes from the approximate latitude of San Diego. ❈

DIVISION 23 BREWING

7408 Trade St., San Diego, CA 92121
858-752-1925 • division23brewing.com

Wed.-Fri. 3-9 pm;
Sat. noon-9 pm

WHEN DID YOU OPEN?
May 2015.

WHAT ARE YOUR MOST POPULAR BEERS?
Freight Damage IPA.

Danky Gnar Gnar, a big IPA with a light body that is bursting with tropical fruit aromas thanks to massive late additions of American, Australian, and New Zealand hops.

Spray Tan Coconut Brown Ale is a malty chocolate brown ale with 100 percent organic toasted coconut added.

Sour Superintendent Berliner Weisse: Lemon on the nose and a great tart finish, our classic Berliner Weisse is an easy drinking summer beer for all. Great on its own, or you can become a mixologist with one of our ten different flavored syrups.

WHICH BEERS ARE YOU PROUDEST OF?
We are extremely proud of our Sour Superintendent Berliner Weisse. Division 23 was one of the very first breweries in San Diego to craft this sour style, and the very first to offer a multitude of syrup options. We won a medal for this beer at the 2015 Cal. State Fair. This beer has served as a craft beer entry point for many patrons that might otherwise have not ordered a beer.

HAVE YOUR BEERS WON ANY AWARDS?
Our Sour Superintendent Berliner Weisse has won two awards! It won silver at the 2015 Cal. State Fair and gold at the 2016 SD International Beer Competition!

WHAT ARE THE BIGGEST CHALLENGES YOUR BREWERY HAS FACED?
Brewing enough beer to keep all

tap handles live. Sourcing hops for small breweries without long-term hop futures contracts can be very challenging and costly.

ARE YOU DOG & FAMILY FRIENDLY?

Yes! We even have dog treats for when we get a special guest.

DO YOU HAVE FOOD?

We do not serve food; Pauly's Pizza is happy to deliver. Occasionally we do have a food truck; we post to Instagram whatever delicious truck is serving that day.

WHAT ELSE CAN YOU TELL US?

Our Training Wheels IPA was named when cofounder Kellen Smith told then-assistant brewer Eric that it was time for him to "take off the training wheels and brew his own IPA." The training wheels have indeed come off.

One of Kellen and Allen's first beers that they brewed together prior to the creation of Division 23 Brewing was named Binder Clip IPA because they had to use office stationery to hold the air-lock on the carboy that continuously blew off due to pressure. The Binder Clip recipe has since been retired.

"50 Divisions" is the most widely used standard for organizing specifications and other written information for commercial and institutional building projects in the United States and Canada. Division 23 in the construction industry relates to heating, ventilation, and air conditioning (HVAC).

Division 23 Brewing has a private and secret room that is often used by local San Diego celebrities who enjoy visiting craft breweries and want to maintain a certain measure of privacy.

Division 23 Brewing is the only known brewery in Southern California to exclusively use all-organic glassware. ❋

39

20

INTERGALACTIC BREWING CO.

9715 Carroll Centre Rd., #107, San Diego, CA 92126
858-750-0601 • intergalacticbrew.com

Mon.–Fri. 3–9 pm;
Sat. & Sun. 1–8 pm

WHEN DID YOU OPEN?
2013.

WHAT ARE YOUR MOST POPULAR BEERS?
The Cake Is a Lie, a coffee cream ale, and Space Oasis, a coconut porter.

WHICH BEERS ARE YOU PROUDEST OF?
Our oatmeal stout and American wheat. They're incredibly easy to drink, and classic styles.

HAVE YOUR BEERS WON ANY AWARDS?
We have won 34 awards over the last four years for 18 different beers at the LA International Beer Competition, the Cal. State Fair Commercial Beer Competition, and the SD International Beer Festival.

WHAT ARE THE BIGGEST CHALLENGES YOUR BREWERY HAS FACED?
Raising capital to go through the expansions and growth that we want to see.

WHAT'S THE ATMOSPHERE LIKE?
We most regularly are cited as being laid-back, welcoming, and friendly. We are very much a bunch of nerds here, with a love of sci-fi and science, so we have fun with that.

ARE YOU DOG & FAMILY FRIENDLY?
Yes and yes.

DO YOU HAVE FOOD?
Nope, just food trucks.

WHAT ELSE CAN YOU TELL US?
We originally started on an 18-gallon system in 1,200 square

feet of industrial space. Pretty stupid.

We won our first gold medal for the eighth beer we brewed, two months after we opened.

Our May the 4th Be With You event is our busiest day of the year; we have Star Wars art galleries, light-saber fighting, and, of course, themed beer. ❇

21

LONGSHIP BREWERY

10320 Camino Santa Fe, Suite C, San Diego, CA 92121
858-246-7875 • longshipbrewery.com

Tues.-Thurs. 3–8 pm;
Fri.– Sun. noon–10 pm

WHEN DID YOU OPEN?
July 2016.

WHAT ARE YOUR MOST POPULAR BEERS?
Our best-selling beers are our Shieldwall IPA and our Loki's Wit Witbier. We change our beers out regularly, though, so our top seller changes each month depending on what was recently released.

WHICH BEERS ARE YOU PROUDEST OF?
I would say that we are most proud of our dopplebock, Ragnabock. Aside from being our first award-winning beer, the style is rare among the huge number of San Diego breweries and requires some degree of skill to create the beer successfully, which the award shows that we have.

HAVE YOUR BEERS WON ANY AWARDS?
Ragnabock won a silver medal at the New York International Beer Festival in 2016.

WHAT ARE THE BIGGEST CHALLENGES YOUR BREWERY HAS FACED?
We faced many challenges on our three-year quest to open our doors and during our first couple of years of business. Finding a location, hiring the right contractor, and coordinating equipment purchases all proved difficult at first. Currently, we are faced with the challenge of making ourselves known and visible in an area that is very resistant to signage and visibility.

WHAT'S THE ATMOSPHERE LIKE?
We strive to create a welcoming, relaxed atmosphere where people can come, have a drink,

and socialize with friends. We have ample seating, mainly in the form of long tables, and plenty of board games. We modeled our tasting room after a Scandinavian longhouse to create a place of communal gathering and interaction. My two favorite phrases that people have used to describe us have been "welcoming" and "clean."

ARE YOU DOG & FAMILY FRIENDLY?

Both. We even have dog training classes every Saturday at noon.

DO YOU HAVE FOOD?

No food is available, though we are looking to partner up with food trucks.

WHAT ELSE CAN YOU TELL US?

The Viking helmets and shields around the brewery were all handmade by friends and staff.

We intentionally do not have televisions in order to avoid the background distractions that come with them, allowing people to truly focus on why they came: other people. ❊

LONGSHIP BREWERY

SAN DIEGO, CA

North County, San Diego

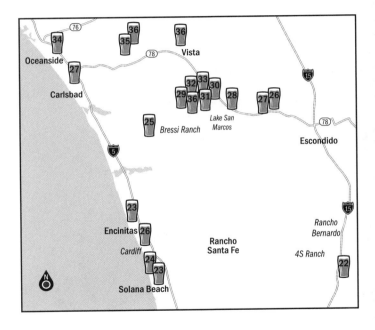

22. Second Chance Beer Co., San Diego
23. Culture Brewing Co., Solana Beach
23. Culture Brewing Co., Encinitas
24. Pizza Port, Solana Beach
25. Burgeon Beer Co., Carlsbad
26. Lost Abbey, Cardiff
26. Lost Abbey, San Marcos
27. Mason Ale Works, San Marcos
27. Mason Ale Works, Oceanside
28. Rip Current Brewery, San Marcos
29. Iron Fist, Vista
30. Booze Brothers, Vista
31. Barrel Harbor, Vista
32. Aztec Brewing Co., Vista
33. Ebuillition Brew Works, Vista
34. Bagby Beer Co., Oceanside
35. Horus Aged Ales, Oceanside
36. Belching Beaver Brewery, Oceanside
36. Belching Beaver Brewery, Vista
36. Belching Beaver Tavern, Vista

SECOND CHANCE

Brewery and taproom, 15378 Ave. of Science, Suite 222, San Diego, CA 92128
858-705-6250 • secondchancebeer.com

Mon. 4–8 pm; Tues.–Thurs. 2–9 pm;
Fri. & Sat. noon–11 pm; Sun. noon–7 pm

Beer lounge, 4045 30th St., Suite A, San Diego, CA 92104
619-487-1470 • secondchancebeer.com

Mon. 4–8 pm; Tues.–Thurs. 3–10 pm;
Fri. & Sat. noon–midnight; Sun. noon–8 pm

WHEN DID YOU OPEN?

The brewery opened in July 2015.

WHAT ARE YOUR MOST POPULAR BEERS?

Seize the IPA, Mulligan, Tabula Rasa, and Legally Red.

WHICH BEERS ARE YOU PROUDEST OF?

Tabula Rasa toasted porter, because it won double-gold back-to-back years at the Great American Beer Festival. Our understanding is this has only happened one other time in the whole history of the competition, and that was by Firestone Walker. We're in great company there! Generally, I'm proud of all of our beers, though, because they are consistently well made, balanced, dry-finished, and without defects. Not many breweries can claim all of those qualities.

HAVE YOUR BEERS WON ANY AWARDS?

In addition to Tabula Rasa, Legally Red Hoppy American Red (named after me, a red-headed, fiery attorney, by my husband and our brewmaster, Marty) also took a silver at the GABF.

Mulligan Irish-Style Red won a silver at the San Diego International Beer Fest. Marty has amassed more than a dozen GABF medals, six World Beer Cup medals, and countless other local medals.

WHAT ARE THE BIGGEST CHALLENGES YOUR BREWERY HAS FACED?

Permitting with the local and state authorities for our liquor and construction licenses and dealing with a landlord who does not understand our business. As an example, for our initial construction and our expansion, the city essentially extorted us to do public improvement projects as a condition of granting our permitting, but we know it did not do the same when our neighbors—much larger corporations who had money to fight such impositions—did construction projects around the same time.

WHAT'S THE ATMOSPHERE LIKE?

Guests, including our "loyalists" (regulars who come here multiple times a week), tell us there is something unique and special about our taproom. We have a kids corner, an adults only area with adult games such as cornhole and darts, and a first-rate team that strives to give every guest at least one positive, memorable experience every time they visit.

DO YOU HAVE FOOD?

We have a variety of delicious food trucks six days a week.

WHAT ELSE CAN YOU TELL US?

We've had an engagement party, one wedding, and a couple of rehearsal dinners, among countless birthdays and retirement parties, corporate milestone celebrations, and even baby showers and a few two-year-old birthday parties! It really is endearing and warms our hearts that people want to share such special and memorable occasions with us! ✳

23

CULTURE BREWING CO.

Brewery and tasting room: 111 South Cedros Ave., Solana Beach, CA 92075
858-345-1144 • culturebrewingco.com

Mon.–Sun. noon–9 pm

Ocean Beach tasting room: 4845 Newport Ave., Ocean Beach, CA 92107
619-255-3811 • culturebrewingco.com

Mon.–Thurs. & Sun. noon–10 pm; Fri. & Sat. noon–midnight

Encinitas tasting room: 629 South Coast Hwy. 101, Encinitas, CA 92024
760-487-5775 • culturebrewingco.com

Daily noon–9 pm

WHEN DID YOU OPEN?
February 2013 in Solana Beach.

WHAT ARE YOUR MOST POPULAR BEERS?
LA Cerveza is the ultimate summertime beer—lager brewed with a slight hint of Mexican influence. Blonde Ale is a balanced, crisp beer with a light body that is reminiscent of a German-style kolsch. Mosaic IPA is our version of the classic California IPA, with

citrus and herbal characteristics and moderate bitterness.

WHICH BEERS ARE YOU PROUDEST OF?

Keyhole IPA, a rendition of our IPA infused with roasted grapefruit rinds, giving this India pale ale a palette-pleasing citrus, smooth finish. This was a special release in December 2013 for the Grant Brittain/Del Mar Skate Ranch Photo Show. We release it a few times a year until we run out.

HAVE YOUR BEERS WON ANY AWARDS?

GABF 2016 gold medal for the brown ale; GABF 2017 bronze medal for the blonde ale.

WHAT ARE THE BIGGEST CHALLENGES YOUR BREWERY HAS FACED?

What to brew next.

WHAT'S THE ATMOSPHERE LIKE?

Local meetup spot to enjoy good beer with good friends.

ARE YOU DOG & FAMILY FRIENDLY?

Yes to both.

DO YOU HAVE FOOD?

In Solana Beach, Wednesday through Sunday we host local food trucks. We have food vendors daily after 4 pm in Ocean Beach. ❄

24

PIZZA PORT

135 N. Hwy 101, Solana Beach, CA 92075
858-481-7332 • pizzaport.com

Sun.–Thurs. 11 am–10 pm;
Fri. & Sat. 11 am–11 pm

WHEN DID YOU OPEN?
1987.

WHAT ARE YOUR MOST POPULAR BEERS?
Swami's IPA, Chronic Amber Ale, Drivin' Me Hazy IPA.

WHICH BEERS ARE YOU PROUDEST OF?
Our recent outpouring of hazy IPAs. Josh Schaner has been tirelessly improving upon each recipe, and his efforts are obvious by our empty tanks.

HAVE YOUR BEERS WON ANY AWARDS?
Yeah-huh.

WHAT ARE THE BIGGEST CHALLENGES YOUR BREWERY HAS FACED?
The biggest ones came earlier in our existence. Most recently, we have undertaken major efforts to get our beer into new areas. Our sales team are doing an amazing job at that.

WHAT'S THE ATMOSPHERE LIKE?
We love our jobs, we love this company. I wouldn't go anywhere else, and that's not just hyperbole. Cain Reyes, our GM, goes out of his way to make sure that our customers are having the same experience that we are, and he's great at it.

Phrases customers have used to describe the brewery have included "extremely rare" and "impossibly fun."

ARE YOU DOG & FAMILY FRIENDLY?
Yes and yes, but dogs on patio only.

DO YOU HAVE FOOD?
Yep. Pizza, wings, salads, and a few other apps.

WHAT ELSE CAN YOU TELL US?
We are among the oldest of the San Diego breweries, and we have been lucky enough to be the first to put many different powerhouses on draft. The first keg of Stone beer was tapped here, among many others. Pizza

Port has always been proud to support local breweries and to not waste taps on the "big three."

Vince and Gina Marsaglia are still very involved in the day-to-day operations of the company, and they are truly amazing people. Their leadership trickles down to the rest of us, and they trust us to do our jobs and represent their brewery well. If you are looking to find the magic that makes Pizza Port special, you need look no further than the two of them. ✳

BURGEON BEER CO.

6350 Yarrow Dr., Suite C, Carlsbad, CA 92011
760-814-2548 • burgeonbeer.com

Mon. & Tues. 4–8 pm; Wed. & Thurs. 3–9 pm; Fri. 3–10 pm;
Sat. noon–10 pm; Sun. noon–8 pm

WHEN DID YOU OPEN?
December 2016.

WHAT ARE YOUR MOST POPULAR BEERS?
Our IPAs and stouts.

WHICH BEERS ARE YOU PROUDEST OF?
We are very proud of our IIPA Mixed Greens. This beer utilizes six different hop varietals, and it is a recipe that we have been dialing in for many years.

HAVE YOUR BEERS WON ANY AWARDS?
We have entered into two competitions and won gold at both: the SD International Beer Competition for our ESB and the Cal. State Fair for our grissette (Noble Miner).

WHAT ARE THE BIGGEST CHALLENGES YOUR BREWERY HAS FACED?
Our biggest challenge has been strategic growth and deter-mining when to enter certain markets.

WHAT'S THE ATMOSPHERE LIKE?
Burgeon means to grow, so we have a lot of growing plants in our tasting room. The tasting room has almost a Pacific Northwest feel, with 5.5-inch thick cedar bar tops, a 20-foot live wall, and a tree in the middle of the tasting room. People have described our tasting room as beautiful, with a lot of attention to detail, and our beer has been described as clean, full flavored, and not too bitter.

ARE YOU DOG & FAMILY FRIENDLY?
We are dog and family friendly.

DO YOU HAVE FOOD?
We have food trucks Wednesday through Sunday every week. We rotate the food every day. Our complete food truck schedule

can be found on our website.

We chose the name Burgeon because we all grew up in North County San Diego. We have all been friends since high school.

We built out the tasting room ourselves with cedar wood from Julian. All the trees burned down in the cedar fire of 2003. Although the trees died in the fire, the wood under the bark was perfectly preserved. We cut, milled, and created the bar top entirely out of repurposed wood from the fire.

Even though Anthony (partner/our brewer) has been commercially brewing for eight years, he and our partner Derek continued to homebrew for over a decade. ✳

BURGEON BEER CO.

26

THE LOST ABBEY

155 Mata Way, Suite 104, San Marcos, CA 92069
800-918-6816 • lostabbey.com

Mon.-Fri. 1-7 pm;
Sat. & Sun. 11 am-8 pm

2007 San Elijo Ave., Cardiff, CA 92007
lostabbey.com

Mon. noon-9 pm; Tues. & Wed. 11 am-9 pm;
Thurs.-Sat. 11 am-11 pm; Sun. 11 am-4 pm

WHEN DID YOU OPEN?
May 2006.

WHAT ARE YOUR MOST POPULAR BEERS?
Port Wipeout IPA; Lost Abbey Devotion Blonde Ale.

WHICH BEERS ARE YOU PROUDEST OF?
Duck Duck Gooze, a beer that takes three years to make; once you taste it, you know why.

HAVE YOUR BEERS WON ANY AWARDS?
Too many to list.

WHAT ARE THE BIGGEST CHALLENGES YOUR BREWERY HAS FACED?
Brewing in San Diego County with more than 140 breweries adds unique challenges.

WHAT'S THE ATMOSPHERE LIKE?
We're the smallest brewery with the biggest name.

ARE YOU DOG & FAMILY FRIENDLY?
Family friendly in both San Marcos and Cardiff locations; dog friendly only in Cardiff.

DO YOU HAVE FOOD?
We do not, but we allow it to be brought in.

WHAT ELSE CAN YOU TELL US?
We're actually three brands under one roof. The Lost Abbey, Port Brewing, and The Hop Concept. Same brewers, same equipment; we break out which beer goes to which brand based on demographics. ❄

The Lost Abbey
BREWING COMPANY

27

MASON ALE WORKS

R&D brewery: 2002 South Coast Hwy., Oceanside, CA 92054
760-429-7424 • masonaleworks.com

Production brewery: 255 Redel Rd., San Marcos, CA 92078
760-798-8822 • masonaleworks.com

Both locations open at 11:30 daily

WHEN DID YOU OPEN?
2015.

WHAT ARE YOUR MOST POPULAR BEERS?
Jambi IPA, Charley Hustle Red IPA, Cash Imperial Coffee Stout.

WHICH BEERS ARE YOU PROUDEST OF?
Jambi IPA—it's a clean and classic example of a West Coast IPA.

HAVE YOUR BEERS WON ANY AWARDS?
Charley Hustle won gold at the SD International Beer Festival.

WHAT ARE THE BIGGEST CHALLENGES YOUR BREWERY HAS FACED?
Getting noticed among a sea of great breweries in San Diego!

WHAT'S THE ATMOSPHERE LIKE?
We have a very industrial vibe to our space. Lots of steel and reclaimed wood with a touch of fabric to tie it all together. We describe our brewery as "craft built." It represents our ethos of working hard and building our business by hand.

ARE YOU DOG & FAMILY FRIENDLY?
Yes and yes.

DO YOU HAVE FOOD?
Yes. Urge Gastropub is attached; it has an extensive menu of modern pub classics.

WHAT ELSE CAN YOU TELL US?
The name Mason was about the 12th name we came up with; all the others were taken!

Our location in San Marcos is likely the only brewery in California that is overlooked by a bowling alley. ✸

28

RIP CURRENT BREWING

1325 Grand Ave., #100, San Marcos, CA 92078
760-481-3141 • ripcurrentbrewing.com
Mon.-Thurs. 3-8 pm; Fri. 3-9 pm;
Sat. noon-9 pm; Sun. noon-7 pm

Tasting room: 4101 30th St., San Diego, CA 92104
619.793.4777 • ripcurrentbrewing.com

Mon.-Thurs. 3-10 pm; Fri. & Sat. noon-midnight; Sun. noon-10 pm

WHEN DID YOU OPEN?
December 2012.

WHAT ARE YOUR MOST POPULAR BEERS?
Lupulin Lust Double IPA and Off the Lip IPA are the best sellers, but Java Storm Coffee Imperial Porter is a big hit as well.

WHICH BEERS ARE YOU PROUDEST OF?
Breakline Bock is a traditional German-style bock. This is a dark lager and very challenging to make. We have won numerous medals for this beer, including back-to-back gold medals at the Great American Beer Festival!

HAVE YOUR BEERS WON ANY AWARDS?
We frequently win awards for many of our beers at major competitions. For instance, Java Storm won the gold medal at the Los Angeles, San Diego, and Cal. State Fair commercial beer competitions.

WHAT ARE THE BIGGEST CHALLENGES YOUR BREWERY HAS FACED?
Keeping up with demand on our core brands while maintaining nearly 20 different beer styles on tap at all times!

WHAT'S THE ATMOSPHERE LIKE?
Our brewery tasting room is relaxed and emphasizes a casual beer experience. Patrons taste our beers while looking into the main brewery and enjoying our display of nearly 1,500 vintage beer cans from the 1930s to 1960s.

ARE YOU DOG & FAMILY FRIENDLY?

Yes on dog and family at our San Marcos location. Our San Diego location has food, so no pets are allowed.

DO YOU HAVE FOOD?

Our patrons enjoy food from nearby restaurants and food trucks.

WHAT ELSE CAN YOU TELL US?

Our brewmaster was named the 2011 Top Homebrewer in the World by winning the most medals at the largest home-brewing competition. In 2015, Rip Current Brewing won the equivalent for most medals won at the GABF. We don't believe this combo has ever been done before. ❈

IRON FIST

1305 Hot Springs Way, #101, Vista, CA 92081
760-216-6500 • ironfistbrewing.com

Wed. 4–9 pm; Thurs. 3–9 pm; Fri. 3–10 pm;
Sat. noon–10 pm; Sun. 1–8 pm

Tasting room: 1985 National Ave., #1132, San Diego, CA 92113
619-255-5818 • ironfistbrewing.com

Mon-Thurs. 3–10 pm; Fri. & Sat. noon–11 pm;
Sun. noon–8 pm

WHEN DID YOU OPEN?

October 2010.

WHAT ARE YOUR MOST POPULAR BEERS?

Our best-selling in distribution are Renegade Blonde, which is a German-style kolsch; Counter Strike Double IPA, which is made with Citra and Galaxy hops; Nelson the Impaler, an American pale ale made with Nelson hops; and Velvet Glove, our imperial oatmeal stout. In our tasting room, our top seller is Counter Strike, followed closely by Renegade Blonde and Summer City Lager.

WHICH BEERS ARE YOU PROUDEST OF?

That's like asking which is your favorite child. We love all our beers! When we opened, we had four Belgian beers and the kolsch, which was very unusual. Our love for Belgians still burns bright. Our Velvet Glove has won a gold medal, and we are certainly very proud of that! We are also proud of our lighter beers and their consistency—Renegade Blonde and Summer City Lager.

HAVE YOUR BEERS WON ANY AWARDS?

Velvet Glove, gold medal. Spice of Life, bronze medal. We also have won a silver medal for Chocolate Mint Stout, which we brewed in collaboration with Ken Schmidt, and a bronze medal for Aloha Plenty, also brewed in collaboration with Ken Schmidt.

WHAT ARE THE BIGGEST CHALLENGES YOUR BREWERY HAS FACED?

When we opened we were #32 or #33 in San Diego. Now, I believe, there are more than 150. Many of those breweries had lots of capital behind them. We were completely self-funded, so capital has always been an issue. With so many breweries, shelf space and tap handle placement and retention are more and more difficult.

WHAT'S THE ATMOSPHERE LIKE?

We pride ourselves in being *very* friendly. We want you to feel like a great friend even if it is the first time you are in here. Both our tasting rooms are big, comfortable, open areas with indoor and outdoor seating. Someone once said that we were the "huggiest" brewery.

ARE YOU DOG & FAMILY FRIENDLY?

Yes and yes.

DO YOU HAVE FOOD?

In Vista, we usually have a great food truck right outside our door. In San Diego, several fantastic restaurants surround us. People bring in food, and we have a restaurant, Mishmash, that delivers.

WHAT ELSE CAN YOU TELL US?

Over the years, we have had dozens of fundraisers for a variety of causes and charities that have raised thousands of dollars.

We host two food drives a year to feed those in need. In San Diego, we support the local artists and host art shows on a monthly basis. ❆

BOOZE BROTHERS

2545 Progress St., Vista, CA 92081
760-295-0217 • boozebros.com

Mon. 4–8 pm; Tues. & Wed. 4–9 pm; Thurs. 4–10 pm; Fri. 3–10 pm;
Sat. noon–10 pm; Sun. noon–8 pm

WHEN DID YOU OPEN?
October 2013.

WHAT ARE YOUR MOST POPULAR BEERS?
Buena Vista IPA; Ol' Grandaddy's IIPA; Penny Blonde; SunUp Stout with Coffee and Vanilla.

WHICH BEERS ARE YOU PROUDEST OF?
You can't pick a favorite child!

HAVE YOUR BEERS WON ANY AWARDS?
We've won a million awards in our minds and hearts, but zero in the real world.

WHAT ARE THE BIGGEST CHALLENGES YOUR BREWERY HAS FACED?
Organic growth without outside money (but we prefer it that way).

WHAT'S THE ATMOSPHERE LIKE?
Our tasting room is spacious, rustic, and genuine. We have an outside patio, music stage, outside bar, and plenty of room to feel comfortable.

DO YOU HAVE FOOD?
We have food vendors generally every Tuesday through Sunday. Burgers, pizza, tacos, seafood, etc. Just depends on the day!

WHAT ELSE CAN YOU TELL US?
Dave and Donny (the owners) are originally from Sweden but moved here as children. They were homebrewers for five years here in Vista before finally opening up an actual brewery. We've

taken over five suites in our five-year span.

We're all avid skateboarders and are passionate in incorporating the skate, art, and music culture with our brewery.

Ben Horton is our artist for all our branding; he's famous throughout the world for his unique art and the skateboard brand he owns, $lave Skateboards. ✻

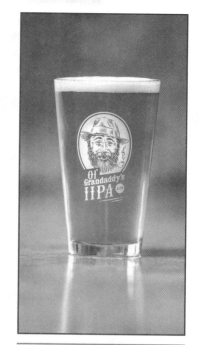

31

BARREL HARBOR

2575 Pioneer Ave., Suite 104, Vista, CA 92081
760-734-3949 • barrelharborbrewing.com

Mon.-Thurs. 3-9 pm; Fri. 3-10 pm;
Sat. noon-10 pm; Sun. 2-7 pm

WHEN DID YOU OPEN?

September 2013.

WHAT ARE YOUR MOST POPULAR BEERS?

Fenris IPA, a West Coast–style IPA, and South Island Pilsner, a dry-hopped German-style pilsner

WHICH BEERS ARE YOU PROUDEST OF?

Really love the pilsner—my personal favorite and go-to beer.

HAVE YOUR BEERS WON ANY AWARDS?

Our Brown Ale took bronze in the 2014 SD International Beer Festival, silver in the California Commercial Craft Brewers Competition, and bronze in the 2016 SD International Beer Festival. Our Rungnir Belgian Dark Strong Ale took gold at the 2017 SD International Beer Festival, beating a Belgian brewery in a Belgian category. ;-)

WHAT ARE THE BIGGEST CHALLENGES YOUR BREWERY HAS FACED?

Attrition of partners. We started out with four, and I am the last man standing.

WHAT'S THE ATMOSPHERE LIKE?

A quaint nautical feel; customers comment on the relaxed atmosphere and the wide variety of great beers available.

ARE YOU DOG & FAMILY FRIENDLY?

Yes.

DO YOU HAVE FOOD?

We try to have food trucks on site on Fridays and Saturdays. ❊

AZTEC

2330 La Mirada Dr., #300, Vista, CA 92081
800-706-6324 • aztecbrewery.com

Mon.–Wed. 3–8 pm; Thurs. & Fri. 3–9 pm;
Sat. 1–9 pm; Sun. 1–7 pm

WHEN DID YOU OPEN?

September 2011.

WHAT ARE YOUR MOST POPULAR BEERS?

Macaroon Nut Brown, Aztec Gold Lager, El Dorado Blonde, Simrillo IPA.

WHICH BEERS ARE YOU PROUDEST OF?

Hmmm. Who's your favorite child? Tough to answer. Personally, I am proud of all our beers, especially the award winners below. My favorite is the Hop Serpent Imperial IPA. Our brewer (Paul Naylor) does incredible work, and this beer is crafted with five hops (Columbus, Cascade, Centennial, Summer, and Galaxy). It's a bright easy-to-drink beer with lots of hop flavor and aroma. Love to see people's reaction when they take a sip.

HAVE YOUR BEERS WON ANY AWARDS?

At the San Diego International Beer Festival, we won gold in 2012 for our Aztec Amber, bronze in 2013 for Aztec Noche De Los Muertos, silver in 2013 for Aztec Amber; silver in 2014 for Robles De Oro (a barley wine); gold in 2014 for Aztec Amber; and gold in 2016 for Funk # Four in the Wood and Barrel Aged Beer category. The Funk # Four was our four-year anniversary beer.

WHAT ARE THE BIGGEST CHALLENGES YOUR BREWERY HAS FACED?

Ruthless, dishonest distributors; a callous landlord; former partners who did not get along with our brewer or us; and increased competition. It's a tough, unforgiving business.

WHAT'S THE ATMOSPHERE LIKE?

Comfortable. Good vibe. Homey feel. It's not a fancy place. We did all the decorations and painting ourselves. We built our own bar. We do all the art (we are still professional designers/artists). We have a lot of live music thanks to our son/partner who is a professional musician.

Do you have food?

Besides pretzels, no. We have food trucks Thursday through Saturday

What else can you tell us?

Aztec is an old brand we are reviving as a modern indie craft brewery. The original brewery was founded in 1921, during Prohibition, in Mexicali, Mexico, by three San Diego businessmen.

Aztec moved to Logan Heights (San Diego) in 1932 and became the third-largest brewery on the West Coast in the 1930s–40s.

Aztec was bought out by the Altes Brewing Company of Michigan in 1948, and the brand was phased out.

We came across the history and brand in 2008 while researching ideas for a line of retro beer-themed apparel and decided it was too cool to just be a T-shirt design. It needed to be resurrected. It took three years of planning, research, and fundraising to get it up and running in 2011.

Aztec has become a well-known local music venue and features live music three nights a week. Our open mic (Thursdays) is one of the best in San Diego and showcases some amazing local talent. We have a PA, amps, mics, and a drum kit so musicians can jump in and play. No karaoke.

Aztec's owners are artists and musicians and do their own labels, website, and merchandise design. ❉

EBULLITION BREW WORKS

2449 Cades Way, Suite D, Vista, CA 92081
760-842-1046 • ebullitionbrew.com

Wed.-Thurs. 3 pm-9 pm;
Sat. noon-10 pm; Sun. noon-8 pm

WHEN DID YOU OPEN?

July 2017.

WHAT ARE YOUR MOST POPULAR BEERS?

The Hazy IPA is the #1 seller, followed by our Bitter Rival IPA and Deli Rye Pilsner.

WHICH BEERS ARE YOU PROUDEST OF?

I am the most proud of our coffee stout and Hazy IPA. The stout already has a few awards, but it's also my personal favorite! I call it my breakfast beer because it is. The Hazy IPA is delicious as well, and because it sells so well, our customers have made me very proud of it.

HAVE YOUR BEERS WON ANY AWARDS?

The coffee stout has won awards.

WHAT ARE THE BIGGEST CHALLENGES YOUR BREWERY HAS FACED?

First, getting open! All the licenses and the build-out were riddled with constant hurdles and new challenges that we had to overcome, but I'm sure that this isn't the first time you have heard this from a brewery owner.

Second, getting people to know that we exist! Social media is huge, but the biggest driver of customers to our place has been word of mouth. I suppose that social media is some form of extension of that, but when a customer comes in and loves the place, they tend to come back with friends.

WHAT'S THE ATMOSPHERE LIKE?

People tend to describe our tasting room as "modern/contemporary" as well as dog and kid friendly. We wanted to set ourselves apart from the common rustic look that most breweries have.

ARE YOU DOG & FAMILY FRIENDLY?

Our brewery is dog and family friendly, with a play area for kids and plenty of games for kids and adults. We also have two water bowls for dogs and doggy treats.

DO YOU HAVE FOOD?

We sell South African meat pies from a local restaurant (the owner delivers them to us), as well as the usual pretzels and mustard that you might find in many breweries. We also try new snacks every once in a while, to see what our customers will enjoy.

WHAT ELSE CAN YOU TELL US?

We have beautiful tap handles that our master brewer Mike Reidy made for us, but we also have a Bottoms Up tap system that fills our pint glasses from the bottom. It uses small half-dollar–sized magnets to seal the bottom of the pint glass; we then hand the magnets out to the customers after they're done with their beer so that they can advertise for us on their fridges or toolboxes or anywhere else they deem necessary to put one. ❋

BAGBY

601 South Coast Highway, Oceanside, CA 92054
760-270-9075 • bagbybeer.com

Mon.–Sat. open at 11 am;
Sun. open at 10 am

WHEN DID YOU OPEN?
September 2014.

WHAT ARE YOUR MOST POPULAR BEERS?
Sweet Ride Bohemian Pilsner, Dork Squad IPA, Zombie Gate Imperial Stout, Continental Cream Ale, Worker Bee Golden Ale with Honey.

WHICH BEERS ARE YOU PROUDEST OF?
All of them! Mostly we're very proud of the sheer number and diversity of beer we brew— something for everyone! We usually have more than 20 house beers on tap.

HAVE YOUR BEERS WON ANY AWARDS?
Yes, Sweet Ride won gold at

GABF, Asphalt Jungle Irish Dry Stout won bronze at GABF, and we've medaled at lots of other smaller local competitions.

WHAT ARE THE BIGGEST CHALLENGES YOUR BREWERY HAS FACED?

Managing the space and ensuring everyone is well attended to (due to the size of our establishment) have been challenges.

WHAT'S THE ATMOSPHERE LIKE?

We are a mid-century BMW dealership turned into a two-story, indoor-outdoor beer compound. Lots of open space, outdoor seating, ocean view. We are usually complimented on our design, layout, and aesthetic, as well as our quality beer and outstanding cocktail program. Usually people are very impressed by the scale of our place, the many seating options, and our fantastic beer, which is brewed by Jeff Bagby, formerly of Pizza Port, and one of the most highly regarded and awarded brewers in the country.

ARE YOU DOG & FAMILY FRIENDLY?

Yes, and yes—both!

DO YOU HAVE FOOD?

Yes! Casual California food: everything from an awesome burger to handmade pizza to the best fish tacos—simple, done well, with the highest-quality ingredients. ✳

HORUS AGED ALES

4040 Calle Platino, Suite 120, Oceanside, CA 92056
horusbeer.com

Sat. noon–5 pm

WHEN DID YOU OPEN?

March 2017.

WHAT ARE YOUR MOST POPULAR BEERS?

Barrel-aged Belgian-style sour ales.

WHICH BEERS ARE YOU PROUDEST OF?

Boss Tycoon, a collaboration imperial stout with J. Wakefield, because it pushed boundaries on what was possible with adjuncts. Up until that point, brewers would experiment with a couple of different adjuncts in one beer, but Boss Tycoon pushed the envelope with eight. It has the most adjuncts in one beer to date. The flavors are all there and easily distinguishable. They include macadamia nuts, coffee, honey, chocolate, marshmallow, vanilla bean, cacao, and coconut. It was considered one of the best beers of 2017 by many.

HAVE YOUR BEERS WON ANY AWARDS?

No, but we won numerous homebrewing medals in the past.

WHAT ARE THE BIGGEST CHALLENGES YOUR BREWERY HAS FACED?

Making the transition from small-scale homebrewing to nearly 100 oak barrels full of

beer, and propagating house yeast culture in large quantities.

WHAT'S THE ATMOSPHERE LIKE?

A big open space filled with wine, whiskey, and other spirits barrels, with lots of room for growth.

Customers have said, "always pushing boundaries," "majestic hall of oak," and "amazing flavors that have not been done before."

ARE YOU DOG & FAMILY FRIENDLY?

Neither.

DO YOU HAVE FOOD?

No.

WHAT ELSE CAN YOU TELL US?

Horus is a side project; I am an accountant for an aerospace company by day.

I made 55 collaboration beers in 2017. Collaborations are a great way to introduce your style of beers into markets and regions that might not have ever seen them otherwise. They are a great way to learn from other brewers, work on something creative with friends, and challenge what is considered possible. The feedback from my collaborations thus far has been both inspiring and rewarding.

The brewery name is an ode to brewer Kyle Harrop's dad, Bob, who has been a falconer since he was 12 years old. In ancient Egypt, Horus was portrayed as the falcon-headed god. Kyle has been around hawks and falcons his entire life, often referring to his dad's birds as his feathered siblings. ✦

BELCHING BEAVER BREWERY

Main production facility/headquarters:
1334 Rocky Point Dr., Oceanside, CA 92056
760-732-1415 • belchingbeaver.com

Original brewery/tasting room: 980 Park Center Dr., Ste. A, Vista, CA 92081
760-599-5832 • belchingbeaver.com

North Park tasting room: 4223 30th St., San Diego, CA 92104
619-223-3116 • belchingbeaver.com

Ocean Beach tasting room: 4836 Newport Ave., San Diego, CA 92107
619-223-3116 • belchingbeaver.com

Tavern and grill (restaurant): 302 East Broadway, Vista, CA 92084
760-295-8599 • belchingbeaver.com

Opening times vary by location; check the website.

WHEN DID YOU OPEN?
October 2012.

WHAT ARE YOUR MOST POPULAR BEERS?
Peanut Butter Milk Stout; Me So Honey Wheat/Blonde Ale; Phantom Bride IPA (collaboration with the Deftones band)

WHICH BEERS ARE YOU PROUDEST OF?
We'd be remiss if we didn't give praise to our Peanut Butter Milk Stout; not many breweries were making this novelty style when we created it during our first year of existence. It was met with overwhelming enthusiasm for its uniqueness, but also its deliciousness. It is so distinctly a peanut butter beer, yet balanced and drinkable—not cloying and overwhelming.

Phantom Bride IPA is an excellent example of growth: to get to work with the fine people that are the Deftones band, to collaborate on a beer together, and for the result to be an insanely delicious West Coast–style IPA (which is quickly catching up to our PB Stout sales)—that is extraordinarily exciting and has helped put us on the map in other places throughout the United States, and even the world.

HAVE YOUR BEERS WON ANY AWARDS?
Yes! Recently we won first place for the second time in the Alpha King Challenge (a hop-forward beer challenge event that is part of GABF). Our Thizz Is What It Is IIPA won in 2017, and our Pound Town IIIPA won in 2014. In 2017, we won two awards in the San Diego International Beer Competition, three in the LA Beer Competition, and five in the North American Brewers Association Beer Competition.

WHAT ARE THE BIGGEST CHALLENGES YOUR BREWERY HAS FACED?
Rapid growth in San Diego County, as well as distribution and keeping up with demand. (A great problem!) We recently went through a brand refresh, which was time-consuming and rather expensive, but we were so happy with its reception. Refining our logo and slogan has been hugely beneficial in reaching more people!

WHAT'S THE ATMOSPHERE LIKE?
"Dam good times!" We want to brew beer for everybody, and we also want them to have a great time drinking it! We're all about good times with good friends and family, which we think should be enjoyed with a dam (that's a beaver pun!) good brew. While our motto is to have a good time and to make beer fun again, we are serious about our craft, and we will never compromise on quality.

ARE YOU DOG & FAMILY FRIENDLY?
Vista brewery, Oceanside, North Park, and OB: yes; tavern restaurant: patio only.

DO YOU HAVE FOOD?
Our tavern in downtown Vista does; it's upscale bar food. Chef Ramiro is insanely talented, and he works with a local high school to help students learn to grow their own food, which we also use for some of our produce.

WHAT ELSE CAN YOU TELL US?
One hundred percent of our tasting rooms are managed and run by women (so is our canning line!), another fact we are proud of in this typically male-dominated industry.

In hop-head saturated San Diego, whose inhabitants are extraordinarily fond of big IPAs, we set out to popularize the milk stout. While we've won some big accolades for our IPAs, the several delicious stout options, not exactly the norm here in SD, helped set us apart. ✳

Orange
County

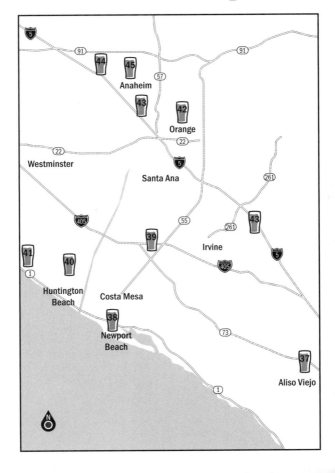

STADIUM BREWING CO.

26731 Aliso Creek Rd., Aliso Viejo, CA 92656
949-448-9611 • stadiumbrewing.com

Sun.-Thurs. 11 am-midnight;
Fri. & Sat. 11 am-2 am

WHEN DID YOU OPEN?

2000. Did a complete remodel in 2015.

WHAT ARE YOUR MOST POPULAR BEERS?

We have 60 taps, and we call them "rotating" because we are constantly bringing in new and fun beers! We have it all. We carry on average seven to ten of our own brews at any given time, and the most popular beer of ours is our Stadium Blueberry Lager (it comes with real blueberries in it).

WHICH BEERS ARE YOU PROUDEST OF?

I would say our blueberry lager. It started out as a seasonal beer and was so popular and in such high demand we had to make it a permanent beer. Our brewmaster Greg Schneider worked on our Stadium Sours for 15

months or so. They are very unique and delicious.

HAVE YOUR BEERS WON ANY AWARDS?

Not necessarily, but we often attend the Brew Ha Ha festivals, and our blueberry lager is very well known and sought out; we always sell out of that one!

WHAT ARE THE BIGGEST CHALLENGES YOUR BREWERY HAS FACED?

I would have to say staying current and fresh with the constant changing of the beer trends. Being a brewery and having to maintain our beers as well as the 60 rotating taps, and keeping them up to date and current with trends poses a problem at times.

WHAT'S THE ATMOSPHERE LIKE?

We are a blend of craft brewery and sports bar; we have a great menu that has something for everyone; and we have two large

sunny patios that face the Town Center Fountain and Park, so we are very kid friendly. Locals refer to our staff as the "brew crew," and we have staff shirts with the slogan.

ARE YOU DOG & FAMILY FRIENDLY?
Family friendly.

DO YOU HAVE FOOD?
Yes! We have an in-house executive chef, Aaron Knigge, and his menu has everything from brewery pretzel bites and buffalo wings to great salads and sandwiches, as well as some special-

ties like chicken risotto, Greek tacos, and cedar-planked salmon. We also have prime rib on the weekends. And we have rotating specials that change every two weeks and are always a hit! ✻

NEWPORT BEACH BREWING CO.

2920 Newport Blvd., Newport Beach, CA 92663
949-675-8449 • nbbrewco.com

Mon. & Tues. 5–11 pm; Wed. & Thurs. noon–11 pm; Fri. noon–1 am;
Sat. 9–1 am; Sun. 9 am–11 pm

WHEN DID YOU OPEN?

April 1995.

WHAT ARE YOUR MOST POPULAR BEERS?

Newport Blonde and our rotating IPA.

WHICH BEERS ARE YOU PROUDEST OF?

Newport Blonde—we have been able to perfect a recipe that is highly drinkable without sacrificing true "craft" flavor.

HAVE YOUR BEERS WON ANY AWARDS?

We've won multiple medals over the years. Our most distinguished include one gold, two silvers, and three bronzes at GABF, as well as a silver in the World Beer Cup.

WHAT ARE THE BIGGEST CHALLENGES YOUR BREWERY HAS FACED?

Prior to opening in 1995, our city was concerned about the impact a brewery would have. They cited concerns about the potential for the smell of beer being brewed, the impact of traffic, early morning pickups and deliveries, etc. After opening, some local residents were con-

cerned about the potential for noise being made late at night by our customers.

ARE YOU DOG & FAMILY FRIENDLY?
Yes, both.

DO YOU HAVE FOOD?
Yes, and many different types. Everything from wood-fired pizzas and burgers to jambalaya and fresh salmon. We also have a breakfast/brunch menu that is available on Fridays and Saturdays.

WHAT ELSE CAN YOU TELL US?
We opened our doors on April 1st, April Fools' Day.

We opened the doors as Newport Beach Brewing Company, but once we opened, we started being known as "BrewCo" and that has stuck. ✺

GUNWHALE ALES

2960 Randolph Ave., Unit A, Costa Mesa, CA 92626
949-239-9074 • gunwhaleales.com

Sun.–Wed. 11 am–11 pm;
Thurs.–Sat. 11 am–8:30 pm

WHEN DID YOU OPEN?

Late 2016.

WHAT ARE YOUR MOST POPULAR BEERS?

Bait Ball, an unfiltered IPA; Pau Brah! IPA; Majordomo, a citrus farmhouse ale; Hopped for Mama, a farmhouse IPA; Barno, a rye saison dry-hopped with Nelson.

WHICH BEERS ARE YOU PROUDEST OF?

Bait Ball IPA is a crowd pleaser, so we have ended up brewing it the most. It is a balanced, lighter-bodied, and lower-bitterness IPA that is very drinkable. But we are quite proud of the many saisons and farmhouse beers we have made. We are proud to offer a changing list of seasonal beers, with exciting yeast strains (some wild), artisan malts, local fruits and herbs . . . and we are working on very balanced beers that exhibit terroir and are exemplary of the life and place and people who live here. We are proud of Barno, Hopped for Mama, Chickabiddy—Hoppy Table Beer, and Flooded Fields, a summer saison with California wild rice. These are examples of innovative and hybrid-style beers that reflect the farmhouse tradition but with a very West Coast expression.

HAVE YOUR BEERS WON ANY AWARDS?

We are pretty new to this, but we won silvers for Shellmaker, an oyster dry stout, and for Old Rackatee, a farro saison, at the Cal. State Fair.

WHAT ARE THE BIGGEST CHALLENGES YOUR BREWERY HAS FACED?

Gunwhale was started small (10-BBL batches) and lean, by three friends who were outsiders to the industry. We feel very humbled by the response we have received, and we are struggling to make enough beer right now to meet demand. Southern California is very expensive, and our county has an extremely tight industrial market with high costs. Finding enough production space and organizing the timeline to open a new facility is intense. The capital required is much higher here than elsewhere, and regulations are not always so easy to navigate.

WHAT'S THE ATMOSPHERE LIKE?

Our brand is anchored by a local taproom that is a place that not only offers better beer product but also acts as a "third place" in the community. It is coastal and farmhouse inspired, which coheres with our approach to beer making. Other than the chairs, we built every detail in it ourselves, from hand-drawn and -painted murals and signs to woodworking and tables and antique elements. It is very relaxed and hip without pretension. We have no TVs, but we do have an analog Scrabble-letter beer menu, and we play well-curated music. It is an environment that strives to nurture meaningful interaction and ideas. Instead of adding to the noise, we promote collaboration, constructive discourse, and transparency, with hopes to bring along the community on our beer-making adventure.

ARE YOU DOG & FAMILY FRIENDLY?

Yes, friendly to both.

DO YOU HAVE FOOD?

We have partnered with food trucks and local restaurants to supply our customers.

WHAT ELSE CAN YOU TELL US?

"Gunwhale" is a name inspired by a prior era. It means the top ridge of a boating vessel (now more commonly known as a gunnel), derived from the place where a gun is attached to a ship in order to fend off threats. We think our name is a curious, unique, and memorable one, but we were most inspired by its use in the Old West. "Loaded to the gunwhales" meant overflowing and was slang for having tipped back a few too many fermented beverages.

Our brand icon is a whale vertebrae, and it reminds us of the rustic coast (which we have experienced from northern California to Baja California), where such remains are often washed ashore.

We hired Alex Tweet of Fieldwork Brewing to help us dial in plans and some of our pilot batches on our Sabco Brew Magic homebrewing system, and we will always be grateful for his help at that critical time. ❉

40

FOUR SONS

18421 Gothard St., Suite 100, Huntington Beach, CA 92648
714-584-7501 • foursonsbrewing.com

Mon.–Thurs. 4–9 pm; Fri. & Sat. noon–9 pm;
Sun. noon–8 pm

WHEN DID YOU OPEN?
September 2014.

WHAT ARE YOUR MOST POPULAR BEERS?
CocoNutorious Coconut Amber Ale, The Great One Imperial IPA, Land of Hopportunity Blood Orange IPA.

WHICH BEERS ARE YOU PROUDEST OF?
Special K is a sour blonde that we brew with black currants. We brew it as often as we can (bi-monthly), and it always sells out immediately. It is an extremely tasty sour that will definitely catch up on you at almost 8 percent.

HAVE YOUR BEERS WON ANY AWARDS?
Many. O'Sonset, our Irish red, has won multiple gold medals at various competitions around the country. Many of our other beers have won gold/silver/bronze awards.

WHAT ARE THE BIGGEST CHALLENGES YOUR BREWERY HAS FACED?
The biggest challenge we have had (and probably most breweries have it too) is deciding when and how to expand. When you're selling a lot of beer and need an increase in production, it's always tough to decide when is right, where the funding will come from, how and where to expand, and most importantly, if you even should.

WHAT'S THE ATMOSPHERE LIKE?
Our family created the brewery and taproom to be a place that we would want to hang out at, since that is all we ever did before the brewery. We wanted to create a laid-back environment where people could come in and enjoy themselves, be relaxed, drink some good beer, meet new friends, watch sports, everything they could do in a bar but this would be a more chill environ-

ment. A lot of customers refer to us as their "Cheers," where they become friends with everyone and we all know their names.

DO YOU HAVE FOOD?

We have rotating food trucks out back Wednesdays through Sundays.

WHAT ELSE CAN YOU TELL US?

We are 100 percent family owned and operated. Myself, my three brothers, and my parents all work full time here (seven days a week) and you will definitely see us working behind the bar. You will also see our wives and children running around every day as well!

We are all huge hockey fans and have all played our whole lives, so our taproom evolved into an LA Kings bar, as we play every game on all our TVs with surround sound! We are huge fans of variety in our beers, so we typically try to release one to two new beers every week. ❄

41

RIIP BEER COMPANY

17216 Pacific Coast Highway, Huntington Beach, CA 92649
714-248-6710 • riipbeer.com

Mon.–Fri. & Sat. 11 am–10 pm;
Sun. 11 am–8 pm

WHEN DID YOU OPEN?
October 2015.

WHAT ARE YOUR MOST POPULAR BEERS?
Super Cali IPA, Raider Bob Double IPA, DanK IPA, Wake & Bake Coffee Stout.

WHICH BEERS ARE YOU PROUDEST OF?
Super Cali IPA—we won a silver medal at the GABF in the American IPA category. It was our first year at GABF, and we won in the most competitive category. This put us on the map.

HAVE YOUR BEERS WON ANY AWARDS?
Yes. Super Cali IPA, 2016 GABF silver medal; DanK IPA, 2015 Taste of Huntington Beach gold; DanK IPA, 2017 silver at San Diego International Beer Festival; DanK IPA, 2017 silver at Taste of Huntington Beach; Tastes Waves IPA, 2017 bronze at Taste of Huntington Beach.

WHAT ARE THE BIGGEST CHALLENGES YOUR YOUR BREWERY HAS FACED?
Keeping up with demand.

What's the atmosphere like?

We are on the PCH, and we are known for being the super chill surf and skate beach bum brewery. Very easy going, reggae music vibe. Many of our customers just got done surfing out front. It is seat-yourself-and-relax, with picnic tables and old vintage pics of HB on the wall. We are rooted to the old HB surf town vibe.

Are you dog and family friendly?

Yes, we always have kids and dogs.

Do you have food?

We do not serve food, but right next door are several locations of some super bomb food: Super Mex (Mexican food), Tsunami Sushi (teppan and sushi), Golden Olive (pizza, Mediterranean, and pasta), Secret Spot (notorious health bomb food; don't let the "healthy" fool you), and Subway.

What else can you tell us?

We deliver beer to homes. Yep, growlers, crowlers, bottles, kegs. That is because at first we did not have a taproom, so the only way to get our beer for our first six months of existence was through delivery. And to make it even crazier, it was in a 1931 Helms Bakery coach, which kinda looks like a trolley train. ✳

42

CHAPMAN CRAFTED BEER

123 N. Cypress St., Orange, CA 92866
844-855-2337 • chapmancrafted.beer

Mon.–Thurs. 4–10 pm; Fri. & Sat. noon–midnight;
Sun. noon–8 pm

When did you open?

August 2016.

What are your most popular beers?

Hello Again Lager, Slow Riser Nitro Red Ale with Coffee, and our rotating IPA series.

Which beers are you proudest of?

To be honest, this is like choosing your favorite child. We make it a point to be proud of every beer we turn out. We make such a variety of beers that each day one beer makes sense and the next day another beer hits the spot.

Have your beers won any awards?

Not yet.

What are the biggest challenges your brewery has faced?

Keeping up with demand.

What's the atmosphere like?

Our most common feedback is that our tasting room has a mellow, chill vibe that is welcoming for all ages.

Are you dog & family friendly?

Yes and yes.

Do you have food?

We have beef jerky and chips and salsa on-site, and rotating food trucks.

What else can you tell us?

Our head brewer, Brian Thorson, is a former brewer at Drake's Brewing Company and Trumer. We love making all kinds of lagers. ❊

43

BACKSTREET BREWERY

1884 S. Santa Cruz St., Anaheim, CA 92805
657-236-4050 • backstreetbrew.com

14450 Culver Dr., Suite E., Irvine, CA 92604
949-857-0160 • backstreetbrew.com

15 Main St., #100, Vista, CA 92083
760-407-7600 • backstreetbrew.com

For hours, refer to website

WHEN DID YOU OPEN?

Irvine, 1998; Vista, 2004; Anaheim, 2015.

WHAT ARE YOUR MOST POPULAR BEERS?

Jagged Lil Pilsner, Rita Red Ale, Tomahawk DIPA, Set Sail IPA.

WHICH BEERS ARE YOU PROUDEST OF?

Late to the Party Citra IPA because it is the best damn beer I have ever had.

HAVE YOUR BEERS WON ANY AWARDS?

Yes. We have won 10 Cal. State Fair medals, including a Best of Show for our Jagged Lil Pilsner.

WHAT ARE THE BIGGEST CHALLENGES YOUR BREWERY HAS FACED?

Distribution.

WHAT'S THE ATMOSPHERE LIKE?

Anaheim: laid-back warehouse production brewery with tasting room; Irvine: neighborhood microbrewery; Vista: neighborhood microbrewery with full bar and kick-ass patio.

ARE YOU DOG & FAMILY FRIENDLY?

Anaheim, yes; Irvine and Vista, restricted to patio.

DO YOU HAVE FOOD?

Anaheim, no; Irvine and Vista, pizza, salads, sandwiches, pasta, appetizers.

WHAT ELSE CAN YOU TELL US?

We are not associated with the Backstreet Boys. ✻

TOWNE PARK BREWING CO.

1566 W. Lincoln Ave., Anaheim, CA 92801
714-844-2492 • towneparkbrew.com

Mon.–Thurs. 4–10 pm; Fri. 4–11 pm;
Sat. & Sun. noon–midnight

WHEN DID YOU OPEN?
September 2017.

WHAT ARE YOUR MOST POPULAR BEERS?
Towne isn't defined by any one individual beer. Each of our beers has its own unique personality and characteristics. Each brings its own flavor to the world; this is what builds and sets our beers apart. Each beer in our line is developed with a particular profile, a unique character, always adding something diverse to our lineup. Our most popular beers are our blonde ale, American lager, IPA, white ale, pale ale, and amber ale.

WHICH BEERS ARE YOU PROUDEST OF?
It's almost impossible to pick out just one style that we are proudest of, as each of our beers has its own distinct following and personality. Of all of our highly drinkable beers, our American lager is considered a classic among our customers. Its rich, full-flavored smoothness

| BLONDE ALE | AMERICAN LAGER | INDIA PALE ALE | WHITE ALE | PALE ALE | AMBER ALE |

is crafted from two side-sitting 60-BBL lager tanks.

HAVE YOUR BEERS WON ANY AWARDS?

Yes, our white ale has won Best Beer at the Festival of Ales in Anaheim.

WHAT ARE THE BIGGEST CHALLENGES YOUR BREWERY HAS FACED?

Opening a 30-BBL brewhouse has its own unique set of challenges. We must work tirelessly to maintain our consistency and high standards in production to keep up with our sales and to remain ahead of our production schedule.

WHAT'S THE ATMOSPHERE LIKE?

We designed our brewery in the spirit of community. We created a space to welcome our local patrons and tourists from around the world. As you walk into our brewery, a lively and inviting experience greets you. We offer private tours, live music, and private event spaces that have hosted some of Southern California's top events.

ARE YOU DOG & FAMILY FRIENDLY?

Yes, we are dog friendly and family friendly. We welcome all two-legged and four-legged friends.

DO YOU HAVE FOOD?

We have partnered and collaborated with top local Orange County food trucks and well-known catering services that offer unique menus based on the day.

WHAT ELSE CAN YOU TELL US?

Towne Park originated from one of Orange County's most unique destinations, Rancho Las Lomas, a landmark and wildlife foundation for endangered animals set on 32 acres hosting weddings, events, charitable foundations, and other unique experiences.

Brett Lawrence, Towne Park owner and founder, has a white tiger named Lily. She inspired our white ale.

The Towne Park logo, nostalgic and timeless, originated as an antique street sign positioned in the heart of Rancho Las Lomas that became a symbolic inspiration for our brand's icon.

Our brand logo's original home was located off Route 66. ✻

ANAHEIM BREWERY

336 S. Anaheim Blvd., Anaheim, CA 92805
714-780-1888 • anaheimbrew.com

Mon.-Thurs. 5-9 pm (Memorial Day to Labor Day);
Sat. noon-11 pm; Sun. 1-7 pm

WHEN DID YOU OPEN?
1870–1920, and again in 2011.

WHAT ARE YOUR MOST POPULAR BEERS?
Anaheim 1888 and Anaheim Hefeweizen.

WHICH BEERS ARE YOU PROUDEST OF?
La Morena Mexican Style Dark Lager was inspired by a painting by Chris Maya. *La morena* means "the brunette." The name matches the beer's reddish-bronze color. The painting portrays la morena in traditional *china poblana*, from the era when what is now called Anaheim was part of Rancho San Juan Cajon de Santa Ana.

Anaheim Oktoberfest Lager is brewed according to a 100-year-old recipe, shared by co-owner Greg Gerovac's first brewery boss, Chris Buckley. As an apprentice, Chris found the recipe in an old leather notebook

in a basement of the Paulaner Brewery in Munich. Greg and Barbara Gerovac developed the recipe to suit modern brewing and malting techniques. The resulting beer has a rich, caramel maltiness, balanced with a touch of German Hersbrücker hops and a smooth, slightly toasty finish.

HAVE YOUR BEERS WON ANY AWARDS?
Our Anaheim 1888 has won medals in the LA International Commercial Beer Competition

and the Cal. State Fair Commercial Craft Beer Competition. Our 2015 Anaheim Dark Scotch Ale won bronze in the Scottish-Style Ale category in the LA International Commercial Beer Competition.

WHAT ARE THE BIGGEST CHALLENGES YOUR BREWERY HAS FACED?

Parking is always tight. Fortunately, valet is a very reasonable three dollars.

WHAT'S THE ATMOSPHERE LIKE?

There's a large, shady beer garden where you can kick back with a pint and watch the Disneyland fireworks burst on the horizon. The tasting room feels like a neighborhood tavern. We pride ourselves on excellent service.

ARE YOU DOG & FAMILY FRIENDLY?

Dog and family friendly.

DO YOU HAVE FOOD?

No.

WHAT ELSE CAN YOU TELL US?

The original Anaheim Brewery opened in 1870. It had three sets of owners at three locations in downtown Anaheim before closing when Prohibition became law. Alas, none of those buildings exists today. Greg and Barbara Gerovac kept with tradition by opening in a fourth location in 2011.

Don't miss one of our signature food and music events such as Founder's Day, Sausage Fest, and Oktoberfest. ❈

Los Angeles County

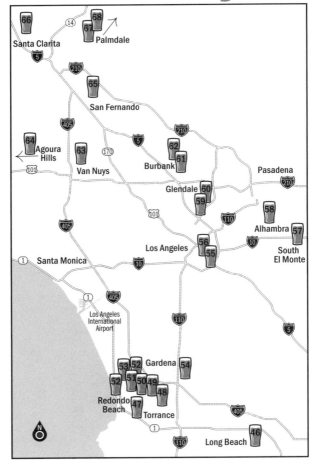

46. Belmont Brewing Co., Long Beach

47. Zymurgy, Torrance

48. Yorkshire Square Brewery, Torrance

49. Strand Brewing Co., Torrance

50. Absolution Brewing Co., Torrance

51. Scholb Premium Ales, Torrance

52. King Harbor Brewing Co., Redondo Beach

52. King Harbor Brewing Co., Redondo Beach

53. HopSaint Brewing Co., Torrance

54. Phantom Carriage Brewery, Gardena

55. Indie Brewing Co., 2350 E. Sunrise St., Los Angeles

56. Arts District Brewing Co., 828 Traction Avenue, Los Angeles

57. Progress Brewing, South El Monte

58. Ohana Brewing Co., Alhambra

59. Frogtown Brewery, 2931 Gilroy St., Los Angeles

60. Eagle Rock Brewery, 3056 Roswell St., Los Angeles

61. Brewyard Beer Company, Glendale

62. Verdugo West Brewing Co., Burbank

63. Macleod Ale Brewing Co., Van Nuys

64. Ladyface Ale Companie, Agoura Hills

65. San Fernando Brewing Co., San Fernando

66. Pocock Brewing, Santa Clarita

67. Transplants Brewing Co., Palmdale

68. Lucky Luke, Palmdale

46

BELMONT BREWING CO.

25 39th Pl., Long Beach, CA 90803
562-433-3891 • belmontbrewing.com

Mon.–Fri. 11:30 am–11:30 pm;
Sat. & Sun. 10 am–11:30 pm

WHEN DID YOU OPEN?
June 1990.

WHAT ARE YOUR MOST POPULAR BEERS?
Blondes, pale ales, IPAs.

WHICH BEERS ARE YOU PROUDEST OF?
We are proud of all our beers!

HAVE YOUR BEERS WON ANY AWARDS?
Strawberry Blonde, Marathon Blonde, and Top Sail Amber Ale.

WHAT ARE THE BIGGEST CHALLENGES YOUR BREWERY HAS FACED?
Our brewery is quite small; we do great with what we have, but it doesn't allow us

to grow much more in terms of production.

WHAT'S THE ATMOSPHERE LIKE?

A homey bar feel on the inside, but we have a breathtaking patio with gorgeous views of Long Beach!

ARE YOU DOG & FAMILY FRIENDLY?

Family friendly; service dogs only.

DO YOU HAVE FOOD?

Yes, traditional American.

WHAT ELSE CAN YOU TELL US?

Oldest brewpub in LA County. Best view of Long Beach. ❊

ZYMURGY

22755 Hawthorne Blvd., Torrance, CA 90505
310-791-1015 • zymurgybrewworks.com

Tues.–Thurs. 3–9 pm; Fri. 3–10 pm;
Sat. noon–10 pm; Sun. noon–6 pm

WHEN DID YOU OPEN?
October 2016.

WHAT ARE YOUR MOST POPULAR BEERS?
Planet Caravan Hibiscus Golden Ale; Chunky Boy Stout; Riviera Flyer Four Finger Johnny Pale Ale; Riviera Flyer on the Wagon DIPA.

WHICH BEERS ARE YOU PROUDEST OF?
All of them, because we take exceptional care and apply great creativity to every beer we brew.

HAVE YOUR BEERS WON ANY AWARDS?
Not yet.

WHAT ARE THE BIGGEST CHALLENGES YOUR BREWERY HAS FACED?
Opening. Overcoming all the bureaucratic BS.

WHAT'S THE ATMOSPHERE LIKE?
Cool place to sit and have a beer while watching us or our customers brew.

DO YOU HAVE FOOD?
No.

ARE YOU DOG & FAMILY FRIENDLY?
We love dogs but cannot allow them in our brewery due to the close proximity to our brewing equipment.

WHAT ELSE CAN YOU TELL US?
We are LA's only nanobrewery that offers customers the opportunity to come in and brew their own beer. ❉

Est. 2015

Zy

Zymurgy Brew Works & Tasting Room
Torrance, CA

YORKSHIRE SQUARE BREWERY

1109 Van Ness Ave., Torrance, CA 90501
424-376-5115 • yorkshiresquarebrewery.com

Wed. 4 pm–11 pm; Thurs.–Sun. noon–11 pm

WHEN DID YOU OPEN?
May 2017.

WHAT ARE YOUR MOST POPULAR BEERS?
We currently have 13 beers plus beer cocktails available in the tasting room. Our most popular beers are the hand-pulled, cask-conditioned ales. They are very smooth and flavorful. Most popular are Early Doors, a pub bitter; The Tenant, an English pale ale; and Wuthering Stout, an oat stout.

WHICH BEERS ARE YOU PROUDEST OF?
Early Doors, pub bitter; The Jonathan, porter; Castle Dangerous, export stout.

HAVE YOUR BEERS WON ANY AWARDS?
We have been awarded with the Cask Marque Certificate of Excellence for our entire cask ale program. The brewery is the second establishment in California to receive this honor and the seventeenth in North America since the program's introduction into the territory. This prestigious certification recognizes the high standards necessary for a great cask ale program. Twice a year, an assessor randomly checks all available cask ales for temperature, taste, appearance, and aroma. All beers must reach the required standard for the establishment to pass, and only then will the bar maintain its accreditation.

What are the biggest challenges your brewery has faced?

Our biggest challenge has been balancing the use of space at the brewery. As we grow, we need more beer production equipment as well as more storage space. At the same time, the tasting room is getting busier. We have already expanded our brewery space and will likely do so again to meet our growth needs.

What's the atmosphere like?

Our tasting room is intimate and reminds many customers of a British pub. Most of our beers are sessionable, with relatively low ABV. Many customers are amazed by how much flavor a beer can have without needing a high alcohol level.

Are you dog & family friendly?

Both dog and family friendly.

Do you have food?

We will be opening our kitchen serving modern British pub food later in 2018. In the meantime, we have food trucks most days we are open.

What else can you tell us?

Many customers believe British beer is warm, and they are pleasantly surprised when they discover that not to be the case. British beer is traditionally served at cellar temperature and is refreshingly cool.

The Queen is often seen in the tasting room and is happy to have a photo taken with customers.

Even though it's never really cold in Southern California, there is usually a group sitting in front of the fireplace in the tasting room or around the fire pit on the patio when the evening is a little chilly. ❈

49

STRAND BREWING CO.

2201 Dominguez St., Torrance, CA 90501
310-429-4444 • strandbrewing.com

Tues.–Fri. 4–9 pm;
Sat & Sun. noon–9 pm

WHEN DID YOU OPEN?

2009.

WHAT ARE YOUR MOST POPULAR BEERS?

24th Street Pale Ale, Atticus IPA, Beach House Amber.

WHICH BEERS ARE YOU PROUDEST OF?

24th Street Pale Ale. It's a classic ale, grapefruit notes abound, slight bitter finish.

HAVE YOUR BEERS WON ANY AWARDS?

White Sand Imperial IPA: gold medal at the LA International Festival; 24th Street Pale Ale: bronze medal at the SD International Beer Festival.

WHAT ARE THE BIGGEST CHALLENGES YOUR BREWERY HAS FACED?

Growing pains.

WHAT'S THE ATMOSPHERE LIKE?

Fun, friendly atmosphere; beer-hall style. People can always meet and talk here as there are no televisions.

ARE YOU DOG & FAMILY FRIENDLY?

Yes and yes.

DO YOU HAVE FOOD?

We use various food vendors on Thursdays, Fridays, and Saturdays (and summer Sundays). The list changes monthly.

WHAT ELSE CAN YOU TELL US?

Strand Brewing was the first production brewery in Torrance and the South Bay.

We are 100 percent independently owned by the two founders, Joel Elliott and Rich Marcello. ❋

ABSOLUTION BREWING CO.

2878 Columbia St., Torrance, CA 90503
310-490-4860 • absolutionbrewingcompany.com

Mon.-Thurs. 4-9 pm; Fri. 2-10 pm;
Sat. 11 am-10 pm; Sun. noon-6 pm

WHEN DID YOU OPEN?
2013.

WHAT ARE YOUR MOST POPULAR BEERS?
Holy Cow Milk Stout, Angel's Demise IPA, Wicked Triple IPA, and whiskey and bourbon barrel-aged delights.

WHICH BEERS ARE YOU PROUDEST OF?
Our ADJD whiskey barrel–aged IPA and Holy Cow Milk Stout were rated "must-buys" by a national publication.

HAVE YOUR BEERS WON ANY AWARDS?
Medals for Angel's Demise IPA, Holy Cow Milk Stout, Strawberry Saison, Kelpie Scottish

ABSOLUTION BREWING COMPANY

PURE PLEASURE ◆ NO GUILT
2878 COLUMBIA ST. TORRANCE, CA 90503 (310) 490 4860

HOLY CA-COW MILK STOUT

ABSOLUTION BREWING COMPANY

Ale, Anniversary Ale, Old St. Bart's, Wassail, Shelby Snakebite Lager, John Bullington English Bitter, and Darkened Angel Black IPA.

WHAT ARE THE BIGGEST CHALLENGES YOUR BREWERY HAS FACED?

Crafty big beer pretending to be craft. You can taste the difference when your pint is handmade, not by a massive industrial machine.

WHAT'S THE ATMOSPHERE LIKE?

Industrial chic! Sit in the brewhouse amongst the fermenters and enjoy the aromas of a live brew. Fun games room to enjoy with a handmade beer—water, grain, yeast, and hops—that's it, no additives, chemicals, or preservatives. Saving the world from bad beer, one pint at a time.

ARE YOU DOG & FAMILY FRIENDLY?

Yes and Yes. Family fun/games room. We brew our own non-alcoholic root beer and cream soda that kids (and parents) love (much lower sugar)! Free doggie treats are made from our spent grain from brewing.

DO YOU HAVE FOOD?

Food trucks; barbecue, wood-fired pizza; sushi Thursdays, gourmet tacos, and more.

WHAT ELSE CAN YOU TELL US?

The pews that provide our taproom seating once accommodated those seeking a very different kind of absolution!

Many of our regulars are dogs who drag their owners in for our dog treats—we even had one who came in on his own skateboard!

Our youngest visitor was less than 12 hours old on the way home from the maternity unit. (Which is why we make and sell Absolution onesies!)

We love working with local restaurants and creative chefs by pairing our beer with their food—German sausages, sushi, luxury chocolates, even Girl Scout cookies. There is nothing that isn't better without a glass of absolution. ✳

SCHOLB PREMIUM ALES

2964 Columbia St., Torrance, CA 90503
424-350-7303 • DrinkScholb.com

Wed. 4–9 pm; Thurs. 3–10 pm; Fri. 1–10 pm

WHEN DID YOU OPEN?
The permit was signed off and we opened in March 2016.

WHAT ARE YOUR MOST POPULAR BEERS?
Tall, Dank & Handsome IPA is by far the most popular in the tasting room and in keg sales. We have a wide variety of IPAs and traditional styles of beer to cover all tastes.

WHICH BEERS ARE YOU PROUDEST OF?
Tall, Dank, & Handsome IPA because it's a great IPA, people love it, and it won second place in a festival out of 100 IPA entries.

HAVE YOUR BEERS WON ANY OTHER AWARDS?
Going Rouge Roggenbier, first place, rye beer, SD International Beer Festival 2017.

#PROST!

order one of me" is a frequently heard quote when guys want to order the Tall, Dank, & Handsome IPA.

ARE YOU DOG & FAMILY FRIENDLY?

Very dog and kid friendly. Dog treats, water bowls. Board games, giant Jenga, and cornhole games for kids.

DO YOU HAVE FOOD?

We schedule food trucks and caterers for food on a weekly basis.

WHAT ELSE CAN YOU TELL US?

We often host

WHAT ARE THE BIGGEST CHALLENGES YOUR BREWERY HAS FACED?

Starting a brewery is a difficult process with a lot of licensing and city inspections. With so many breweries, it's not the slam dunk it used to be. There is a slow growth phase to get the taproom to fill out and to push keg sales, so you need a lot of working capital. We made it past the first year, but it was close. Now we are slowly showing a profit.

WHAT'S THE ATMOSPHERE LIKE?

Family friendly. Very nice bar staff. Big and open feel. "I'll

one-year-old birthday parties for happy parents. At a recent party, we set up a tent in the brewery to contain the little ones.

We often host open brew days for customers to tour the brewery and learn the process.

Our brewer has a BS in chemical engineering from UCSB —very fitting for a beachside party school grad to start a brewery. ✳

52

KING HARBOR BREWING CO.

Brewery tasting room: 2907 182nd St., Redondo Beach, CA 90278
310-542-8657 • kingharborbrewing.com

Mon. & Tues. 4–9 pm; Wed. & Thurs. 4–10 pm; Fri. 2–10 pm;
Sat. noon–10 pm; Sun. 12–6 pm

Waterfront tasting room: 182 International Boardwalk, Redondo Beach, CA 90277
310-374-1400 • kingharborbrewing.com

Mon.-Wed. 3–8 pm; Thurs. 3–10 pm;
Fri. & Sat. noon–midnight; Sun. noon–8 pm

WHEN DID YOU OPEN?
April 2014.

WHAT ARE YOUR MOST POPULAR BEERS?
Tiki Hut IPA, Sink with California Pale Ale, South Bayern Hefeweizen.

WHICH BEERS ARE YOU PROUDEST OF?
Tiki Hut IPA, a big tropical hop flavor/aroma, low bitterness, malt backbone that complements the hop profile.

HAVE YOUR BEERS WON ANY AWARDS?
King Swirly the 3rd, South

Bayern Hefeweizen, Cerveza Hermosa Lager.

What are the biggest challenges your brewery has faced?

Not drinking all the beer ourselves.

What's the atmosphere like?

Beers for the laid-back beach life.

Are you dog & family friendly?

Both, yes.

Do you have food?

No, but we have food trucks Wednesday through Saturday.

What else can you tell us?

Head brewer Phil McDaniel came from Stone (brewer) and The Bruery (lead brewer) before King Harbor.

A good amount of our beer names are based on classic Southern California punk bands.

It is possible to fish from our waterfront tasting room bar. ❋

KING HARBOR
BREWING COMPANY

Redondo Beach, California

HOPSAINT BREWING CO.

5160 West 190th St., Torrance, CA 90503
310-214-HOPS • hopsaint.com

Mon.–Sat. open at 11:30 am;
Sun. open at 10 am

WHEN DID YOU OPEN?

December 2015.

WHAT ARE YOUR MOST POPULAR BEERS?

IPAs are usually the number one seller.

WHICH BEERS ARE YOU PROUDEST OF?

We are most proud of our classic German ales and lagers, as well as our hop-driven IPAs and pale ales.

HAVE YOUR BEERS WON ANY AWARDS?

Yes! Pure Intention Pale Ale won a gold at the 2016 SD International Beer Competition (American pale ale) and a silver at the 2017 GABF (international-style pale ale).

WHAT ARE THE BIGGEST CHALLENGES YOUR BREWERY HAS FACED?

Some of the biggest challenges are staying relevant and in demand with the ever-changing craft beer landscape, as well as financing expensive brewery expansions to keep up with production needs.

WHAT'S THE ATMOSPHERE LIKE?

Our brewery/restaurant has a midcentury-modern-café-meets-industrial feel. We included custom handmade wood features such as four community tables, taster flight holders, and tap handles, all made from recycled skateboard decks.

ARE YOU DOG & FAMILY FRIENDLY?

Family friendly; service dogs only, we are a restaurant.

DO YOU HAVE FOOD?

We serve handmade, fresh, and farmers market sourced (personally selected three times a week) food with an emphasis on real wood-fire cooking and barbecue.

We use white oak to smoke our ribs, brisket, pork, and more, in addition to using our wood-fired stone oven and grill for our menu items.

WHAT ELSE CAN YOU TELL US?

HopSaint supports local businesses and breweries and serves only independent beer as defined by the guidelines laid forth by the Brewers Association. This is important to the survival of small craft beer as well as to educate customers on the impact their choices have when buying beer.

We are extremely passionate about the quality, freshness, and service our customers receive and want to be the best at what we do.

Brewmaster Brian Brewer started homebrewing at age 17, completed UC Davis' Master Brewers Program class of 2003, and has brewed for multiple breweries, including Stone Brewing in Escondido. ❈

PHANTOM CARRIAGE

18525 S. Main St., Gardena, CA 90248
310-538-5834 • PhantomCarriage.com

Mon. 3–10 pm; Tues.–Thurs. 11:30 am–10 pm; Fri. 11:30 am–midnight;
Sat. noon–midnight; Sun. 11 am–6 pm

WHEN DID YOU OPEN?

December 2015 (soft opening); March 2016 (grand opening).

WHAT ARE YOUR MOST POPULAR BEERS?

#1. Broadacres, a wild Berliner Weisse.

#2. Lugosi, a dark, sour quad.

#3. Deadly Harvest, a barrel-aged blonde sour with boysenberries.

WHICH BEERS ARE YOU PROUDEST OF?

I would have to say Lugosi, named in honor of the legendary actor Bela Lugosi (Dracula). It's a big, wine-barrel–aged, sour quad that was in development for over half a decade on the homebrew level. When the family got wind that we named a beer in Bela's honor, and embraced and supported the beer, we worked out a licensing agreement to be the official Bela Lugosi beer.

We age many of our beers in a diverse assortment of wine and spirit barrels obtained through close relationships with regional producers and fermented with cultures developed and fine-tuned over years of trials and research.

We attempt to expand on traditional European brewing and blending techniques using the driving curiosity and dynamic problem solving that stems from our homebrewing roots.

WHAT ARE THE BIGGEST CHALLENGES YOUR BREWERY HAS FACED?

As any small (growing) business, properly managing cash flow; being aware of the various markets (and changes); and hiring the right, motivated staff that vibes with the message/ethos of our brewery's diverse ecosystem.

PHANTOM CARRIAGE
Brewery and Blendery

ARE YOU DOG & FAMILY FRIENDLY?

Our taproom cannot allow dogs due to food safety restrictions. Service animals being the exception, with proof of a certified license. We have an on-site eatery that allows all ages into our establishment. We should forewarn you that we do play heavier metal and screen classic R-rated horror films in our brewery's theater in the late afternoons/evenings, but generally keep our daytime screenings relatively family friendly.

DO YOU HAVE FOOD?

Our key component is fresh food. Our menu features house-smoked meats and a small cafe-style food menu. We have a variety of sandwiches and appetizers that pair well with any of our beer offerings.

WHAT ELSE CAN YOU TELL US?

Our taproom (nestled off the 405 & 110 freeway interchange) is in a warehouse that was transformed into a speakeasy-like taproom, with dark gray walls lined with filled oak barrels. Our dim-lit atmosphere is also accompanied by an on-site 130-inch movie theater featuring cult-classic horror and vintage slasher films.

The brewery building itself may be haunted. Too many weird n' creepy moments late at night once the taproom is closed and the production side is gone for the day. We're planning to bring in a ghost hunter in the near future to get to the bottom of this business.

Phantom Carriage, in name, pays homage to the 1921 Swedish horror film *The Phantom Carriage*. The film was one of the first—if not the first—to incorporate special FX, and has been an inspiration for countless filmmakers, including Bergman and Kubrick. ❋

INDIE BREWING CO.

2350 E. Sunrise St., Los Angeles, CA 90023
323-354-4285 • indiebrewco.com

Tues.–Thurs. 4–10 pm; Fri. 4–11 pm;
Sat. 1–11 pm; Sun. 1–6 pm

WHEN DID YOU OPEN?
December 2015.

WHAT ARE YOUR MOST POPULAR BEERS?
IPA Del Rey; Pacific Kolsch Highway.

WHICH BEERS ARE YOU PROUDEST OF?
All of them, because they are our children.

HAVE YOUR BEERS WON ANY AWARDS?
Yes. Pacific Kolsch Highway—LA International Beer Festival bronze 2016 and 2017; Omally's Irish Stout—LA International Beer Festival silver 2017.

WHAT ARE THE BIGGEST CHALLENGES YOUR BREWERY HAS FACED?
Getting all the licensing needed in a notoriously difficult city to start a business.

WHAT'S THE ATMOSPHERE LIKE?
Our brewery and taproom are

all in one. The taproom sits in between our cold storage and brew floor. The environment is one of a full brewery immer-

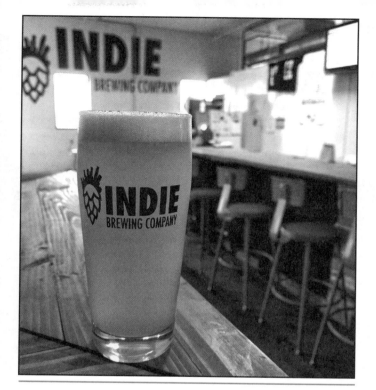

sion, with couches, games, picnic tables, and sports on the screen. Our favorite customer phrases are "chill" and "laid-back."

ARE YOU DOG & FAMILY FRIENDLY?

Yes, kid and dog friendly!

DO YOU HAVE FOOD?

We work with local independent food trucks and vendors and have food available the majority of days we are open. We do not have our own kitchen.

WHAT ELSE CAN YOU TELL US?

Two of our cofounders are from about three miles apart from each other in Scranton, PA. They had never met each other until we started getting the business together.

All the cofounders are 5'7". Weird.

We don't brew pilot batches. The first time we brew a new beer, we brew a full production batch. ❋

ARTS DISTRICT BREWING CO.

828 Traction Ave., Los Angeles, CA 90013
213-519-5887 • artsdistrictbrewing.com

Mon.–Thurs. 3 pm–midnight; Fri. 3 pm–2 am;
Sat. noon–2 am; Sun. noon–midnight

WHEN DID YOU OPEN?
December 2015.

WHAT ARE YOUR MOST POPULAR BEERS?
Traction IPA and Mateo Golden Ale.

WHICH BEERS ARE YOU PROUDEST OF?
Our aurora series, fruited sour program.

HAVE YOUR BEERS WON ANY AWARDS?
GABF 2016, silver medal, Cowboy Curtis Smoked Porter; San Diego Fair 2016, gold medal, Scotch Ale; and a few in LA and California fairs in 2016 and 2017.

WHAT ARE THE BIGGEST CHALLENGES YOUR BREWERY HAS FACED?
Bottling on a medium scale; the brewery being on multiple levels; winning over our residential neighbors; and fostering a sense of community.

WHAT'S THE ATMOSPHERE LIKE?
Playful.

DO YOU HAVE FOOD?
Yes, fried chicken and pub food by Fritzi Coop.

WHAT ELSE CAN YOU TELL US?
We're located in the former home of Crazy Gideon's Electronics Emporium; he's still the landlord.

We also carry liquor and have fun boilermaker pairings with our beers.

We have a great selection of games, most notably 15 lanes of Skeeball (on restored vintage machines). Monday nights are Free Skee Nights with the purchase of a house beer! ✻

PROGRESS BREWING

1822 Chico Ave., South El Monte, CA 91733
626-552-9603 • progress-brewing.com

Mon.–Thurs. 3–9 pm; Fri. 3–11 pm;
Sat. 3–10 pm; Sun. noon–8 pm

WHEN DID YOU OPEN?
August 2013.

WHAT ARE YOUR MOST POPULAR BEERS?
Cavalry DIPA, Blonde, Frida Pale Sour, Electrodome Wheat Wine.

WHICH BEERS ARE YOU PROUDEST OF?
Vincent—it tastes similar to Rodenbach Grand Cru, the best beer in the world.

HAVE YOUR BEERS WON ANY AWARDS?
We do not enter competitions.

WHAT ARE THE BIGGEST CHALLENGES YOUR BREWERY HAS FACED?
Constant expansion and still not being able to keep up with tasting room demand.

WHAT'S THE ATMOSPHERE LIKE?
You can find all kinds of people at our tasting room from all backgrounds.

DO YOU HAVE FOOD?
We have food trucks on Thursdays, Fridays, and Saturdays.

WHAT ELSE CAN YOU TELL US?
We built all of our tanks and, so far, we have not found any leaks.

We do not distribute; you can find our beer only at our tasting room. ✻

PROGRESS
BREWING
SOUTH EL MONTE, CALIFORNIA

58

OHANA BREWING CO.

7 S. 1st St., Alhambra, CA 91801
626-282-2337 • ohanabrew.com

Mon.-Thurs. 4-9 pm; Fri. & Sat. 11 am-10 pm;
Sun. 11 am-5 pm

WHEN DID YOU OPEN?
August 2012 (month of first brew).

WHAT ARE YOUR MOST POPULAR BEERS?
Ohana Pacific Ale (blonde ale); Ohana SpaWater (saison infused with cucumbers and lemongrass); Tiki on the Beach (blonde ale infused with Hawaiian fruit such as papaya and pineapple).

WHICH BEERS ARE YOU PROUDEST OF?
Ohana SpaWater because it is refreshing and unique; we can't keep enough in stock!

HAVE YOUR BEERS WON ANY AWARDS?
Ohana Saison Noir (silver award 2014 World Beer Cup). Other beers that have won awards in commercial beer competitions: Ohana SpaWater (LA Interna-tional Beer Competition 2017); Black Coral (Cal. State Fair Commercial Beer Competition 2017); Saison Kau Wela (SD International Beer Competition 2017).

WHAT ARE THE BIGGEST CHALLENGES YOUR BREWERY HAS FACED?
Permitting and inspection pro-cess in the city of Los Angeles (2.5 years!).

WHAT'S THE ATMOSPHERE LIKE?
Tasting room is laid-back with a Hawaiian vibe.

ARE YOU DOG & FAMILY FRIENDLY?
Family and dog friendly.

DO YOU HAVE FOOD?
Complimentary crackers and pretzels only, but customers are free to bring in their own food.

OUD BRUIN

SOUR BROWN ALE | 1 PINT 6 FL. OZ.
ALC. 7.4% BY VOL.

WHAT ELSE CAN YOU TELL US?

At the time the brewery opened in 2012, owner Andrew Luthi was the youngest brewery owner in the USA.

Brews are supervised by a seasoned former BJs brewer. We have taken in homebrewers, provided training and opportunities to learn and experience commercial brewing, and then watched them go on to other local brewers as head brewers. We are quite proud of that! ✻

www.ohanabrew.com

FROGTOWN

2931 Gilroy St., Los Angeles, CA 90039
323-452-2739 • Frogtownbrewery.com

Wed.–Fri. 5–10 pm;
Sat. noon–10 pm; Sun. noon–8 pm

WHEN DID YOU OPEN?
October 2016.

WHAT ARE YOUR MOST POPULAR BEERS?
Kinky, a blonde ale; Feather It In, a session IPA made with Citra and Mosaic hops.

WHICH BEERS ARE YOU PROUDEST OF?
War on Sobriety, a double IPA that comes in at 10.1 percent ABV and is made with Loral and Mosaic hops.

HAVE YOUR BEERS WON ANY AWARDS?
Not yet!

WHAT'S THE ATMOSPHERE LIKE?
Our brewery is located in an old manufacturing warehouse, so we built our tasting room to complement the industrial vibe. We have a bimonthly rotation of local artists' work showcased on our walls. Everything from the copper bar top to the tables and shelves were hand built by brewery owners Adam Kestel and Mike Voss.

Our customers comment on the low-key, friendly environment of the tasting room. We have a large communal table in the center of the tasting room that encourages people to meet each other and chat over a beer.

ARE YOU DOG & FAMILY FRIENDLY?
Yes, our tasting room is dog and family friendly.

DO YOU HAVE FOOD?
No, but we regularly have food trucks and pop-up food vendors selling food for our customers.

WHAT ELSE CAN YOU TELL US?
Co-owners Adam Kestel and Mike Voss are longtime friends who began brewing small-batch homebrews together on Voss's treetop deck.

Frogtown is the nickname for the neighborhood our brewery

is located in (Elysian Valley). The nickname originated in the 1930s when thousands of small frogs would regularly come up out of the LA River and cover the neighborhood streets like a blanket. Frogs no longer live in the LA River, but the nickname remains. ✿

EAGLE ROCK BREWERY

3056 Roswell St., Los Angeles, CA 90065
323-257-7866 • eaglerockbrewery.com

Tues.-Fri. 4-10 pm;
Sat. noon-10 pm; Sun. noon-8 pm

WHEN DID YOU OPEN?

2009.

WHAT ARE YOUR MOST POPULAR BEERS?

Populist IPA; Manifesto Witbier.

WHICH BEERS ARE YOU PROUDEST OF?

Solidarity (black mild) because it's our flagship beer that we first brewed back in 2009. This beer is not a common style but gets a lot of love from people with the best palates, including brewers and chefs.

HAVE YOUR BEERS WON ANY AWARDS?

Yes.

WHAT ARE THE BIGGEST CHALLENGES YOUR BREWERY HAS FACED?

Opening. It took us more than two years to get through the red tape of opening a brewery in Los Angeles; we were the first brewery to open in the city limits of LA in several decades.

WHAT'S THE ATMOSPHERE LIKE?

Small, family-owned brewery that our customers have described as a "hidden gem." We're

the taproom is very welcoming and well kept.

DO YOU HAVE FOOD?

Just prepackaged snacks like almonds and chips at the brewery. We occasionally have food trucks in the parking lot.

WHAT ELSE CAN YOU TELL US?

We run a monthly women's beer education group that's got a great following, with around 50 attendees every month. ✳

located on a small industrial alley in a nondescript building, yet

BREWYARD BEER COMPANY

906 Western Ave., Glendale, CA 91201
818-409-9448 • brewyardbeercompany.com

Wed.-Thu. 4:30-10 pm; Fri. 4:30-11 pm;
Sat. 1-11 pm; Sun. 1-6 pm

WHEN DID YOU OPEN?
December 2015.

WHAT ARE YOUR MOST POPULAR BEERS?
We created a new category of lagers known as "Common"-style lagers. We also brew Belgian ales.

WHICH BEERS ARE YOU PROUDEST OF?
Our Common-style lagers are uniquely Californian. No other brewery that we know of has dedicated itself to this unique style of beer. We are proud of trying to get this category recognized by the commercial beer world.

HAVE YOUR BEERS WON ANY AWARDS?
Our Jewel City Common has won two awards so far—silver at the SD International Beer Competition in the Amber Lager category and first place in that category at the Cal. Commercial Beer Festival.

WHAT ARE THE BIGGEST CHALLENGES YOUR BREWERY HAS FACED?
We were just home-brewers with a dream. Finding the time and money to build out our brewery ourselves and learning to brew at such a large scale have been challenging.

DO YOU HAVE FOOD?

We have food trucks, restaurant delivery, and BYOF.

WHAT ELSE CAN YOU TELL US?

We have a 1936 Ford flatbed truck in our taproom that you can drink on.

We have a hip-hop karaoke night, paint night, yoga morning, comedy/variety show, an n64 gamer tournament night (monthly), and live music on Saturdays.

A majority of the build-out (especially finish work) was designed and built by the two owners with help from family and friends. ✺

WHAT'S THE ATMOSPHERE LIKE?

Cozy, comfortable, personable, family, mom-and-poppy, cool, unique.

ARE YOU DOG & FAMILY FRIENDLY?

We are both, but family time is more suited for the earlier times of the day.

VERDUGO WEST BREWING CO.

156 W. Verdugo Ave., Burbank, CA 91502
818-841-5040 • verdugowestbrewing.com

Mon.-Thurs. 4-10 pm; Fri. & Sat. noon-10 pm;
Sun. noon-8 pm

WHEN DID YOU OPEN?

January 2017.

WHAT ARE YOUR MOST POPULAR BEERS?

Our two most popular beers are Trustworthy IPA, a West Coast IPA, and Gigil Pils, a puffed jasmine rice lager.

WHICH BEERS ARE YOU PROUDEST OF?

I am very proud of our barrel-aged sour beer program. These are the types of beers I love to drink and love to make. Sour beer is challenging and time consuming to produce, and the payoff is a beer that is unique and very complex.

Have your beers won any awards?

Not yet! We are still new and haven't entered any competitions yet.

What are the biggest challenges your brewery has faced?

Having enough time and fermentation space to brew the variety of beers that we want to share with our customers.

What's the atmosphere like?

The brewery is an inviting, industrial environment for beer lovers to relax in and enjoy a well-crafted pint of beer. We want our guests to feel at home while our friendly employees provide excellent service.

Are you dog & family friendly?

Both. We serve treats and water for dogs and have games for kids and adults.

Do you have food?

Yes, we serve different varieties of pizza, Angus beef burgers, french fries, and crispy calamari.

What else can you tell us?

People have seen a ghost's face in our armoire, but don't worry, he's friendly!

The head brewer has a master of science degree in biochemistry.

We have weekly theme nights such as Vinyl Night Thursdays and Cask Night Fridays. ✻

MACLEOD ALE BREWING CO.

14741 Calvert St., Van Nuys, CA 91411
818-631-1963 • macleodale.com

Mon.-Wed., 5-11 pm; Thurs. & Fri. 5 pm-midnight;
Sat. noon-11 pm; Sun. noon-11 pm

WHEN DID YOU OPEN?
June 2014.

WHAT ARE YOUR MOST POPULAR BEERS?
Better Days Pale Ale, London Lager, The King's Taxes (Scottish 60 shilling cask ale).

WHICH BEERS ARE YOU PROUDEST OF?
Our cask ales because they are delicious and we do them better than anyone in the U.S. and most of Great Britain!

HAVE YOUR BEERS WON ANY AWARDS?
Not yet!

WHAT ARE THE BIGGEST CHALLENGES YOUR BREWERY HAS FACED?
Constant need for money to expand and thrive!

WHAT'S THE ATMOSPHERE LIKE?
Casual, warm, welcoming, friendly. Peanut-shells-on-the-floor kind of place.

ARE YOU DOG & FAMILY FRIENDLY?
Yes, both!

DO YOU HAVE FOOD?
We have daily food trucks. They're the best!

WHAT ELSE CAN YOU TELL US?
We have 8 steel-tip dart boards and sponsor 12 teams in our local darts league.

Until recently, we didn't have any "legitimate" brewing equipment; it was all dairy and wine equipment.

We are bagpipers, and all our beers are named after bagpipe tunes.

We are opening a second location soon, serving all our great beer plus savory meat pies and British pub food, but a better version!

We had a patron who regularly brought her pig, Rosie, but

sadly they moved to Oregon.

We rescued a brewery kitty named Smokey. He'll keep the mice away. We don't have mice, nor will we! ❋

64

LADYFACE ALE COMPANIE

29281 Agoura Rd., Agoura Hills, CA 91301
818-477-4566 • ladyfaceale.com

Open daily at 11:30 am

WHEN DID YOU OPEN?

November 2009.

WHAT ARE YOUR MOST POPULAR BEERS?

Ladyface IPA and La Blonde are the highest-volume sellers, but the hardcore beer fans love Chesebro (imperial) IPA.

WHICH BEERS ARE YOU PROUDEST OF?

Our barrel-aged beers are aged an average of two years and develop very complex flavors from both microorganism and barrel character. Dérailleur Bière-de-Garde and Flamberge Flemish Red are very popular.

HAVE YOUR BEERS WON ANY AWARDS?

We have consistently medaled at LA and SD international beer competitions, as well as the Cal. State Fair. Named *LA Weekly*'s 2013 Best Brewery in LA, and an international RateBeer.com Best Brewpub, Ladyface is known for its award-winning Belgian, French, and American–style ales.

WHAT ARE THE BIGGEST CHALLENGES YOUR BREWERY HAS FACED?

After more than eight years, daily operations are still a challenge. With so many moving parts, there is always something to fix or a fire to put out (figuratively speaking of course!). There is the tendency to forget the early pains of building and opening a brewpub, which is really two separate businesses rolled under one roof. You have all the infrastructure and permitting associated with a brewery and add to that the complexity of getting a restaurant launched. Every government agency wants money from you up-front or takes your firstborn as collateral. We nearly ran out of money getting the doors open, but doing a lot of the work ourselves allowed us to prioritize and reduce expenses.

WHAT'S THE ATMOSPHERE LIKE?

Ladyface is a warm and welcoming, casual European-style brewpub. The ambiance is inspired by the cozy bistros and classic brasseries of Paris and Brussels, and Art Nouveau decor and graphics adorn the interior spaces.

ARE YOU DOG & FAMILY FRIENDLY?

No dogs, but two-legged pets are welcome. We have a great kids' menu for young foodies and a Tin-Tin comic book collection!

DO YOU HAVE FOOD?

The Ladyface menu is rooted in our love of Belgian beer and French brasseries, and our quest to create simple, honest recipes using high-quality ingredients. California versions of European country-style dishes are inspired by seasonal produce, harvests, and farm products that are sustainable and locally grown. Ladyface features its ales in many recipes, and its menu is designed to pair well with the Belgian and French farmhouse-style ales we make. As a brewpub, we have full restaurant and bar services in addition to producing our own beer, and creative, fresh-crafted cocktails are always available.

WHAT ELSE CAN YOU TELL US?

Founded by local residents from Agoura Hills, Ladyface is one of LA County's first revival craft breweries, and the first in the Conejo Valley. Our namesake, Ladyface Mountain, stands behind us at a 2,100-plus feet elevation; it is an impressive gateway to the Santa Monica Mountains; the Ladyface patio offers a scenic view. Ladyface was honored as Agoura Hills' 2015 Business of the Year. In 2014, state senator Fran Pavely awarded Ladyface as the California 27th District's Small Business of the Year for its commitment to the local community. ❀

131

SAN FERNANDO BREWING CO.

425 Park Ave., San Fernando, CA 91325
818-745-6175 • sanfernandobrewingcompany.com

Thurs.–Sun. noon–10 pm

WHEN DID YOU OPEN?

August 2015.

WHAT ARE YOUR MOST POPULAR BEERS?

O'Melveny Red Ale; Grapefruits of Wrath IPA.

WHICH BEERS ARE YOU PROUDEST OF?

The Q-cumber Pale Ale because we were able to bring cucumber, a nontraditional ingredient, to the recipe and have it prominent throughout the flavor profile; Stoney Point Stout because this is a recipe that started it all and continues to be an easy drinking stout.

HAVE YOUR BEERS WON ANY AWARDS?

O'Melveny Red Ale: gold at the SD International Competition, 2016; Marty McRye: silver at the LA International Competition, 2016; Best Brewery in Los Angeles: *Daily News* Readers Poll, 2016 and 2017.

WHAT ARE THE BIGGEST CHALLENGES YOUR BREWERY HAS FACED?

It took us more than a year to find a location that would allow us to build a brewery. Most locations didn't know what a craft brewery was and refused to have a "bar" in their building. We had some major equipment problems immediately after opening the brewery that forced us to replace much of the equipment. In addition to the equipment issues, getting funding for start-up was difficult.

WHAT'S THE ATMOSPHERE LIKE?

Our brewery has a very laid-back attitude. No one is here to judge your taste in beer, and we welcome you with open arms. As a family-run business, we greet you as if we are welcoming you to our home and treat you as part of the community and family. Phrases customer use for us are "the Cheers of the Valley" (everybody knows your name), "hidden gem," and "gathering spot of San Fernando." The following phrase is uttered on a weekly basis by newcomers to the brewery: "I don't know what it is, but there's a feeling about this place that's really cool."

Do you have food?

We do not serve food but are frequented by food trucks on a regular basis.

What else can you tell us?

Our master brewer, Brent Meadows, spent the majority of his career at Firestone Walker Brewing and won numerous awards, including gold medals at GABF.

Our two brewers, Frank and Jose, were some of our first customers and had never brewed before. Now they are vital to each brew and to the everyday operations of the brewery.

We are in the city of San Fernando, in the San Fernando Valley, located just off San Fernando Road.

The city of San Fernando has its own water supply, separate from Los Angeles. The water definitely affects the flavor and ABV of the beer. ✳

POCOCK BREWING

24907 Ave. Tibbitts, #B, Santa Clarita, CA 91355
661-775-4899 • pocockbrewing.com

Wed.-Thurs. 3-9 pm; Fri. 3-10 pm;
Sat. noon-10 pm; Sun. noon-6 pm

WHEN DID YOU OPEN?
December 2015.

WHAT ARE YOUR MOST POPULAR BEERS?
Nuptials, a mango ale; The Old Road, a brown ale; Rooster Pith, an IPA; First 13, a pale ale; Noble Piper, a Scotch strong ale; El Gallo Macho, a Mexican lager with lime zest.

WHICH BEERS ARE YOU PROUD-EST OF?
We are very proud of all of the beers we make. Noble

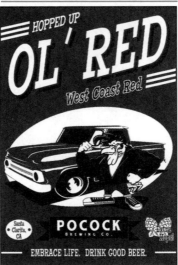

Piper and a few of our barrel-aged beers have won awards from the U.S. Open, LA International, and SD International. Our British Volunteer ESB, Old Road Brown Ale, and One If by Land have been critically well received.

WHAT ARE THE BIGGEST CHALLENGES YOUR BREWERY HAS FACED?
Expansion to keep up with demand. We are currently in an expansion to triple our volume and start with packaged beer.

Wednesday through Saturday. We also allow customers to bring in food.

WHAT ELSE CAN YOU TELL US?

Our heritage is English background meshed with a West Coast style. Our beers range from good examples of styles to combinations of styles and flavors to create new and exciting beers. The atmosphere is fun and friendly, and we are happy to answer any questions a customer may have.

We host live trivia on Wednesday nights, and we have live music on Saturday nights. ✳

WHAT'S THE ATMOSPHERE LIKE?

Very friendly and approachable tasting room and staff. We are here to help introduce the novice craft beer drinker, while at the same time appealing to the discerning palette of the seasoned craft beer fan.

ARE YOU DOG & FAMILY FRIENDLY?

Dog—no; family—yes.

DO YOU HAVE FOOD?

No, but we have food trucks

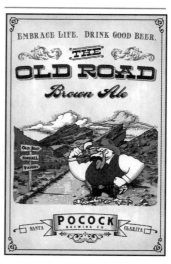

TRANSPLANTS

40242 La Quinta Lane, #101, Palmdale, CA 93551
661-266-7911 • transplantsbrewing.com

Mon. 4–11 pm; Wed. & Thurs. 4–11 pm; Fri. 2 pm–midnight;
Sat. noon–midnight; Sun. noon–9 pm

WHEN DID YOU OPEN?
January 2016.

WHAT ARE YOUR MOST POPULAR BEERS?
El Mas Guapo IPA with Guava;
Filbert Chocolate Hazelnut
Brown Ale; Peaches Be Trippin;
Imperial Peach Ale; CatBirD
IPA with Hop Hash and Hemp
CBD.

WHICH BEERS ARE YOU PROUDEST OF?
We are extremely proud of
CatBirD, our IPA with hop hash
and hemp CBD. We were able
to capture the essence, flavor,
and aroma of hops' cousin cannabis and, unsurprisingly, it's the
clear staff favorite. Our product
is lab tested and THC free. It
has a lab-verified concentration
of CBD, the nonpsychoactive
component in
cannabis that
does not get you
high; it is said to
cause pain relief
and relaxation.

HAVE YOUR BEERS WON ANY AWARDS?
As a young
brewery, we have
yet to rack up
any professional
accolades. We
also know our

weird beers often don't fit neatly into contest-style categories. We received many awards as home-brewers, however.

WHAT ARE THE BIGGEST CHALLENGES YOUR BREWERY HAS FACED?

Just getting open in the first place. It's a long, difficult process that is full of constant challenges. But every brewery has to deal with that.

WHAT'S THE ATMOSPHERE LIKE?

We have a very comfortable, chill vibe in the tasting room. Our wall has a giant mural, and there is art everywhere. We are lucky enough to have an amazing artist on staff. We also have an excellent sound system and a custom music catalog service, which adds to the experience. There are intentionally no TVs.

ARE YOU DOG & FAMILY FRIENDLY?

Yes. Both.

DO YOU HAVE FOOD?

No, but we have packaged snacks and get food trucks as often as we can.

WHAT ELSE CAN YOU TELL US?

The meaning of our logo and name is twofold. Not only is the hop monster (lovingly nick-named "Elvis") transplanting his brain in exchange for hops, all the founders of our company are transplants themselves. We originate from Chicago, New York, and Missouri. Our slogan is "Ales for the Unrooted," which celebrates the melting pot and cultural diversity that is LA.

Transplants Brewing Company is run primarily by a husband-and-wife brewing team, making Transplants part of a short list of breweries owned and operated by a woman. ❈

68

LUCKY LUKE

610 West Ave. O, Suite 104, Palmdale, CA 93551
661-270-5588 • luckylukebrewing.com

Mon.-Thurs. 4–10 pm; Fri. 2 pm–midnight;
Sat. noon–midnight; Sun. noon–8 pm

WHEN DID YOU OPEN?
December 2015.

WHAT ARE YOUR MOST POPULAR BEERS?
Impresario IPA, Millwright Oatmeal Stout, Cartographer Pale Ale.

WHICH BEERS ARE YOU PROUDEST OF?
We believe in quality craft beer and stay close to traditional styles.

HAVE YOUR BEERS WON ANY AWARDS?
Millwright, an oatmeal stout, won gold at the LA International Beer Competition 2016; Scrivener, an American blonde, won silver at the LA International Beer Competition 2017.

WHAT'S THE ATMOSPHERE LIKE?
Rustic; independently owned.

ARE YOU DOG & FAMILY FRIENDLY?
Yes and yes.

DO YOU HAVE FOOD?
No. Customers are encouraged to bring in their own food or eat from our food trucks. ✻

Central Coast

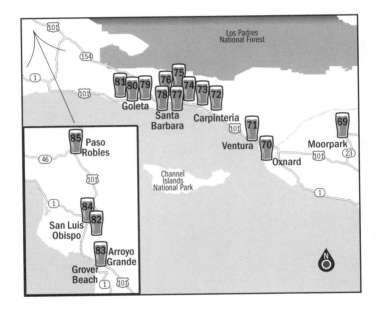

69. Enegren Brewing Co., Moorpark
70. Red Tandem Brewery, Oxnard
71. Leashless Brewing, Ventura
72. Island Brewing Company, Carpinteria
73. brewLAB, Carpinteria
74. Brass Bear Brewing, Santa Barbara
75. Telegraph Brewing Co., Santa Barbara
76. Third Window Brewing, Santa Barbara
77. Topa Topa Brewing Co., Santa Barbara
78. The Brewhouse, Santa Barbara
79. Captain Fatty's Brewery, Goleta
80. M Special Brewing Co., Goleta
81. Hollister Brewing Co., Goleta
82. Bang the Drum, San Luis Obispo
83. ManRock Brewing Co., Grover Beach
84. Underground Brewing Co., San Luis Obispo
85. Firestone Brewing Co., Paso Robles

ENEGREN BREWING CO.

444 Zachary St., #120, Moorpark, CA 93021
805-552-0602 • enegrenbrewing.com

Tues–Thurs. 4–9 pm; Fri. 2–10 pm;
Sat. 11 am–10 pm; Sun. noon–7 pm

WHEN DID YOU OPEN?

July 2011 (founded October 2010).

WHAT ARE YOUR MOST POPULAR BEERS?

Valkyri, a German-style amber; Lightest One, a German-style Helles; Lagertha, a moasic pilsner; Nighthawk, a black lager; The Big Meat, a smoked doppelbock.

WHICH BEERS ARE YOU PROUDEST OF?

Lightest One. We are most proud of this beer because it is a clean, authentic-style German Helles lager.

HAVE YOUR BEERS WON ANY AWARDS?

Yes, we've won awards at the Los Angeles International Commercial Beer Competition in 2013, 2014, 2015, and 2017—in 2017 we won gold for Nighthawk, silver for Big Meat, and bronze for Valkyrie. In 2017, we also won silver for Big Meat at the San Diego International Beer Festival.

WHAT ARE THE BIGGEST CHALLENGES YOUR BREWERY HAS FACED?

As a family-owned and -operated brewery, we face countless challenges on a daily basis, from label design to how to expand efficiently/dealing with space constraints to working on increasing sales. Owning and operating a brewery is wholly a challenge, albeit a really fun one.

WHAT'S THE ATMOSPHERE LIKE?

We have a very open, friendly, and inviting brewery and tasting room with a German theme. No TVs; our brewery focuses on building friendships over a pint of beer.

ARE YOU DOG & FAMILY FRIENDLY?
Yes, both.

DO YOU HAVE FOOD?
We have food trucks daily.

WHAT ELSE CAN YOU TELL US?
We started as homebrewers in the dorm rooms of Loyola Marymount. After graduation, we built a sophisticated home-brew setup that got featured in BYO's "Brew Systems That Make You Drool" column.

We started out as a three-BBL brewery, just the three founders, where we all worked nine-to-five jobs and worked the brewery on nights and weekends. We didn't get much sleep at the time, but we were able to successfully grow our business to our current 15-BBL brewery. ✳

RED TANDEM BREWERY

1009 Harbor Blvd., Oxnard, CA 93035
805-832-4023 • redtandembrewery.com

Wed.-Fri. 4-10 pm;
Sat. 1-10 pm; Sun. 1-7 pm

WHEN DID YOU OPEN?

May 2016.

WHICH BEERS ARE YOU PROUDEST OF?

C-Hag India Pale Ale—Surprisingly fresh, crisp, and smooth, all in one sip. This IPA is named for its hops bill, which includes most every commercially available hop that starts with the letter C, plus Warrior and Amarillo hops. Five total hop additions throughout the brewing and fermenting processes give rise to a wonderful balanced complexity.

Double C-Hag Imperial IPA—this is a serious 10 percent beer that achieves excellent balance with its intense hops load. This beer was partially inspired by potential patrons who telephoned us at the brewery and asked, "What's the highest alcohol beer you have on tap?" We now say, "Double C-Hag, she's a perfect 10." Like her little sister, Double C-Hag is named for her hops bill, which includes most every commercially available hop that starts with the letter C, plus Warrior and Amarillo hops. Five total hop additions throughout the brewing and fermenting processes make this an intense AND sophisticated beer. This beer has been a surprise hit with many wine drinkers who normally do not drink beer.

HAVE YOUR BEERS WON ANY AWARDS?

Double C-Hag DIPA won the #1 IPA award at Surf 'n Suds Carpinteria. Customers love it, my wife loves it, and I love it! Although it's a 10 percent beer, we use an excellent yeast to make it and properly age it, and the result is smooth, not harsh. Apparently, there are a whole lot of 9+ percent ABV harsh beers out there, because I hear about them all the time!

For us, the City of Oxnard has been 99 percent of our challenges. From planning commission to police department to building department to building inspectors, every aspect was an uphill walk to a brick wall. We've even been openly harassed by a high-ranking city official, including harassment of our patrons in our tasting room and use of abusive and profane language with our staffers. We have had to go as far as to pursue a restraining order against the city official. And *no one* knows why she acts as she does. It took us 20 months to open, which included only 4.5 months of construction.

We're chic and modern and homey all at the same time. We've been called the "friendliest brewery in Ventura County" by one of our patrons who visits all of them.

Yes and yes.

Not exactly, but we're right next door to the Pizza Company. Pizza, hot and cold sandwiches, salads, and pasta. They'll bring it in if you let them know you are next door at the brewery. And it's all really good; they've been operating for well over 30 years under the same owner.

We are one block from the beach.

We organize weekly fun bicycle rides in the neighborhood—Sundays at 1 pm.

Our C-Hag IPA is rumored to be named after the brewer's mother, the brewer's next-door neighbor, or the brewer's rabbi—no one is sure which. ❋

LEASHLESS BREWING

585 E. Thompson Blvd., Ventura, CA 93001
805-628-9474 • leashlessbrewing.com

Mon.–Fri. 3–10 pm;
Sat. noon–10 pm; Sun. noon–9 pm

WHEN DID YOU OPEN?
July 2017.

WHAT ARE YOUR MOST POPULAR BEERS?
Sunrise Belgian Blond, V-town IPA, Twinny Dubbel.

WHICH BEERS ARE YOU PROUDEST OF?
All of them! As a certified

organic brewery, it's tough sometimes to source ingredients to make a beer. So when a beer makes it through to the tap . . . well, we are pretty happy!

WHAT ARE THE BIGGEST CHALLENGES YOUR BREWERY HAS FACED?
Getting open was a challenge. We renovated an 87-year-old building historically used for tire repair. Damn, that was opening up Pandora's box. Second, Ventura has a fast-growing beer scene with strong brand loyalty. Making our mark as an organic brewery that focuses on Belgian styles and offering a few gluten-reduced beers is challenging!

WHAT'S THE ATMOSPHERE LIKE?
Relaxed beach vibe with couches, live music, and a TV.

ARE YOU DOG & FAMILY FRIENDLY?
Yes, sir! Our patio is dog friendly

BE ORGANIC

Leashless

BREWING

LIVE FREE

as long as they are on a leash. The whole brewery is family friendly. We have an assortment of games for all ages to enjoy as well!

DO YOU HAVE FOOD?

No, but we have food trucks. Guests can bring in outside food as long as it is packaged in Styrofoam-free containers.

WHAT ELSE CAN YOU TELL US?

We are the first certified green brewery in Ventura and possibly the state!

We've been hosting fund-raisers almost every other week since we first opened.

Leashless is all about surfing without a leash; about being free to cross-step back and forth on a longboard without the constraints of safety. Leashless is all about crafting organic beer, free of inorganic fertilizers and pesticides. ❁

ISLAND BREWING

5049 6th St., Carpinteria, CA 93013
805-745-8272 • islandbrewingcompany.com

Mon.–Thurs. 11 am–9 pm; Fri. & Sat. 11 am–10 pm;
Sun. 11 am–9 pm

WHEN DID YOU OPEN?
2001.

WHAT ARE YOUR MOST POPULAR BEERS?
Avocado Honey Ale, Island

Blonde, Hopliner IPA, and Tropical Lager.

WHICH BEERS ARE YOU PROUDEST OF?
Our national and international award-winning beers show on a

technical level that all the hard work is worth it and resonate with our local beer-tasting crew.

Yes. At the GABF, we won silver in 2002 for our Jubilee Ale, silver in 2004 for our Nut Brown Ale, gold in 2010 for the Barrel Aged Big Island, gold in 2012 for our Starry Night Stout, silver in 2012 for our Barrel-Aged Night Sail, and bronze in 2016 for our Anniversary Ale. At the World Beer Championship, we won gold in 2012 for our Starry Night Stout, platinum in 2015 for our Bourbon Barrel-Aged Big Island Barley-wine, and gold in 2016 for our Anniversary Ale.

WHAT ARE THE BIGGEST CHALLENGES YOUR BREWERY HAS FACED?

Permitting for expansion, construction.

WHAT'S THE ATMOSPHERE LIKE?

Beachy, friendly: we are three blocks from Carpinteria State Beach, right on the train tracks.

DO YOU HAVE FOOD?

No, we have the occasional food trucks, and we are within walking distance of a number of restaurants, so take-out is encouraged. We also have a binder full of local restaurant menus, or you can bring your own.

WHAT ELSE CAN YOU TELL US?

Paul Wright initially got into brewing beer after a stint making wine at home proved too time consuming. His wife, Cheryl, bought him a Mr. Beer brewing kit, and the rest of the family got sucked into the beer-brewing vortex. ❋

brewLAB

4191-8 Carpinteria Ave., Carpinteria, CA 93013
507-319-5665 • brewlabcraft.com

Thurs. 4–9 pm; Fri. 4–10 pm;
Sat. 2–10 pm; Sun. 2–8 pm

WHEN DID YOU OPEN?
September 2014.

WHAT ARE YOUR MOST POPULAR BEERS?
We brew on a 40-gallon system and constantly take the opportunity to brew new things. On average, we release one to three new beers per weekend. We rarely repeat any one beer, and considering we work on a rudimentary, simple system without such tools as glycol, even when we try to re-create a certain beer, it inevitably changes, not to mention we don't always have the exact grains, hops, or yeast on hand, plus the water table changes from season to season.

Having said this, we have a few beers we return to in inexact ways, including but not limited to Red Roots, a ginger red ale; Green Tea IPA, a dry-hopped IPA with a blend of green teas;

Drunken Llama, a chocolaty stout infused with locally roasted coffee beans, bourbon-soaked oak, and vanilla beans; and Llama Saison, a red saison infused with locally roasted coffee beans.

WHICH BEERS ARE YOU PROUDEST OF?
Tough to say. We enjoy all our beers for different reasons and at different times, and because of the constantly evolving nature of our brewing practices, we are hoping we find a new favorite every time we experiment. We have several barrel-aged projects that we are very excited about as well as our gruits (a historic herbal ale using locally foraged flora for bittering and flavoring). We also experiment with local, wild yeast/bacteria and have had many successes. Any time we get to use locally foraged yeast, bacteria, fruit, or any local ingredients, we are momentarily satiated.

HAVE YOUR BEERS WON ANY AWARDS?

None. For many reasons, we haven't submitted a single beer to competition. We may in the future, but for now we are more curious about what our local community thinks of our beer.

WHAT ARE THE BIGGEST CHALLENGES YOUR BREWERY HAS FACED?

Financial. We are very small (we are the owners *and* the brewers, with no equity partners to tell us what to do), which lends itself to many great things, including freedom of creativity in designing how and what we want without the almighty dollar being the driving force behind the decisions we make. Though having the funds to further the level of experimentation we can achieve and to please our simple life needs would be nice, we have been careful not to receive funds from just anywhere and continue to seek funding from what we deem an appropriate place that fits within our holistic goals.

WHAT'S THE ATMOSPHERE LIKE?

Our atmosphere is a key ingredient in the overall experience we want people to feel when they visit. It is an experience that we want to provide, not just a product—beer. Beer is the medium in which we as brewers get to experience and explore our world. We use it as a platform to practice many things, including design/building, woodworking, welding, agriculture, and much more. The physical space was designed and built by us out of mostly salvaged materials, furthering our commitment to reducing our environmental footprint, raising environmental awareness, and being good environmental stewards.

We are also the ones who pour and serve each and every beer, which allows everyone to ask questions about what they are drinking, the ingredients involved, and the processes we go through. This allows for a deeper understanding and an opportunity for deeper connections with our community. We support local agriculture with ingredients; music with live musicians; and artists on our walls.

We have heard people explain our space as cozy and authentic, rustic, and refined.

ARE YOU DOG & FAMILY FRIENDLY?

Both dog and family friendly.

DO YOU HAVE FOOD?

We don't, but we have food trucks every day we are open.

WHAT ELSE CAN YOU TELL US?

While we were starting up the brewery, we lived in our cars and warehouses in order to make ends meet and fully realize our dream. ✿

BRASS BEAR BREWING

28 Anacapa, Unit E, Santa Barbara, CA 93109
805-770-7651 • brassbearbrewing.com

Mon.–Thurs. noon–9 pm; Fri. & Sat. noon–11 pm;
Sun. noon–9 pm

WHEN DID YOU OPEN?
February 2016.

WHAT ARE YOUR MOST POPULAR BEERS?
Hopping Grizzly IIPA; Berry Patch Sour; Holiday Heff.

WHICH BEERS ARE YOU PROUDEST OF?
Our sour is our hardest beer to brew because of the souring process and all the fruit we add. It

took us a few attempts to get it the color we wanted as well, but it is now hitting on all cylinders. The raspberries and blood orange flavors come through really well at the end of the sip in a dry, fruity way.

HAVE ANY OF YOUR BEERS WON AWARDS?
There is a local breweries bracket that happens each year around

March Madness and we always make it to the Final Four, which feels great because we are the smallest brewery in town.

WHAT ARE THE BIGGEST CHALLENGES YOUR BREWERY HAS FACED?

Dealing with permitting and approvals with our city. Santa Barbara makes it nearly impossible to do anything exciting and creative.

WHAT'S THE ATMOSPHERE LIKE?

We are a very small brewery with a very small kitchen, which leads to a very intimate space. Everyone is your friend when you are there, and we offer a special room to the side for kids to hang while parents get to eat and drink.

ARE YOU DOG & FAMILY FRIENDLY?

Yes, we have a special kid activity area.

DO YOU HAVE FOOD?

Yes, all locally sourced from California and most things from Santa Barbara County. A very simple but delicious menu. We have a local cult following for our tri-tip, burgers, and grilled cheeses.

WHAT ELSE CAN YOU TELL US?

We are a husband-and-wife team who started homebrewing in Manhattan, where I was working in finance and my wife in marketing. We decided to quit our jobs, leave NYC, and move back to Santa Barbara to pursue our dreams.

We are hidden in the back of our building, but once you get there you never leave.

Our name came from a hike we did in Glacier National Park, where we came across a family of bears. The way the sun was hitting them that time of day, they glowed brass, hence Brass Bear. ❄

TELEGRAPH BREWING CO.

418 N. Salsipuedes St., Santa Barbara, CA 93103
805-963-5018 • telegraphbrewing.com

Tues.-Thurs. 3-9 pm; Fri. 2-10 pm;
Sat. noon-10 pm; Sun. noon-7 pm

WHEN DID YOU OPEN?
2006.

WHAT ARE YOUR MOST POPULAR BEERS?

White Ale, Variable Frequency IPA, Reserve Wheat Berliner Weisse, Obscura Barrel-Aged Sour Series.

WHICH BEERS ARE YOU PROUDEST OF?

We're particularly proud of our sour beer program. All our sours are distinctive, nuanced, and complex, and use locally sourced, organic fruit.

HAVE YOUR BEERS WON ANY AWARDS?

We have won six GABF medals (two gold, three silver, one bronze) and two World Beer Cup medals (one gold, one bronze).

WHAT'S THE ATMOSPHERE LIKE?

Coastal industrial—exposed beams, reclaimed wood, lots of natural light.

ARE YOU DOG & FAMILY FRIENDLY?

Dog and family friendly.

DO YOU HAVE FOOD?

We do not serve food in-house, but we do work regularly with food trucks here at the tasting room.

WHAT ELSE CAN YOU TELL US?

We are located in a World War II–era Quonset hut, with a translucent polycarbonate façade to bring our coastal California sunshine and fresh air inside.

We have had a sour beer program since 2008.

Telegraph was the first production brewery in Santa Barbara, and we are proud to be a part of a very vibrant craft brewery scene in this area. ❊

THIRD WINDOW BREWING

406 E. Haley St., Santa Barbara, CA 93101
805-979-5090 • thirdwindowbrewing.com

Mon.–Wed. noon–10 pm; Thurs.–Sat. noon–11 pm;
Sun. noon–9 pm

WHEN DID YOU OPEN?
May 2016.

WHAT ARE YOUR MOST POPULAR BEERS?
Lagers, saisons, IPAs, chocolate stouts.

WHICH BEERS ARE YOU PROUDEST OF?
We're proudest of the beers that we are able to make with locally foraged ingredients from the Santa Barbara area.

HAVE YOUR BEERS WON ANY AWARDS?
Not yet, but soon!

WHAT ARE THE BIGGEST CHALLENGES YOUR BREWERY HAS FACED?

Our challenge is figuring out how to make better beer each and every time that we brew.

WHAT'S THE ATMOSPHERE LIKE?

We're a brewery focused on local terroir. We like to think we instill the Santa Barbara vibe in our beers and our atmosphere. We are ever in search of better beer while maintaining a laid-back, California-coast lifestyle filled with good beer, good music, good people, and good times.

DO YOU HAVE FOOD?

We have a restaurant serving locally sourced, chef-driven, and seasonally changing cuisine. It all pairs very well with beer.

WHAT ELSE CAN YOU TELL US?

The name Third Window is based on the story of Santa Barbara, who had a third window installed in her bathhouse tower in honor of the holy trinity. She was later killed for doing this, becoming a saint in the process.

For any of our beers that use fruit or herbs or vegetables, we collect those ingredients from nearby farmers and our customers' backyards. ❋

77

TOPA TOPA

Ventura brewery: 104 E. Thompson Blvd., Ventura CA, 93001
805-628-9255 • topatopa.beer

Mon.–Thurs. noon–9 pm; Fri. & Sat. noon–10 pm;
Sun. 11 am–8 pm

Santa Barbara taproom: 20 Santa Barbara St., Santa Barbara, CA 93101
805-324-4150 • topatopa.beer

Sun.–Wed. 11:30 am–10 pm;
Thurs.–Sat. 11:30–midnight;

WHEN DID YOU OPEN?
June 2015.

WHAT ARE YOUR MOST POPULAR BEERS?
All of our beers do very well, but our best-selling beer is our Chief Peak IPA.

WHICH BEERS ARE YOU PROUDEST OF?
I'm truly most proud of the wide array of beers that our brewers are capable of producing. If I had to pick one, it would be our Howler Coffee DIPA. It is a challenging beer to make and surprises most people when they have it. The hops play well with the light-roast coffee we carefully choose for each batch. It is a fantastic beer that requires thoughtful teamwork to produce.

HAVE YOUR BEERS WON ANY AWARDS?

Our Flatlands saison was awarded a bronze medal in the LA International Beer Festival.

WHAT ARE THE BIGGEST CHALLENGES YOUR BREWERY HAS FACED?

Getting open. Our brew system got delayed for a number of months due to a West Coast port workers union strike. So we almost didn't make it to opening. That was by far our biggest challenge to date. Managing the rapid growth and demand for our beer runs a close second, but that is a challenging and fun aspect of running the brewery.

WHAT'S THE ATMOSPHERE LIKE?

We offer a laid-back, friendly, clean environment for our customers. Our taprooms don't have TVs, and they encourage community and conversation. We have plenty of regulars who tell us that they feel at home at Topa Topa. Our well-trained staff creates a great atmosphere to enjoy brewery fresh beer!

ARE YOU DOG & FAMILY FRIENDLY?

We welcome all well-behaved dogs (on a leash) and children (no leash required).

DO YOU HAVE FOOD?

We don't serve our own food at either location. In Ventura we have food trucks every day of the week, and in Santa Barbara there is a great restaurant called the

Nook that you can order from while enjoying beer in our taproom.

WHAT ELSE CAN YOU TELL US?

We are a 1% for the Planet company. We give back 1 percent of our sales to environmental causes that we believe in. So you can drink beer AND do some good at the same time!

Our brewers are creatures of habit and have a set of rotating music schedules for their work week. Wu-Tang Wednesdays, Salsa/Latin Thursdays, and Diva Fridays are my favorites. Don't be surprised if you hear them blasting Whitney Houston or Dianna while knocking out a brew of Chief Peak.

We are defending winners of the annual pedi-cab races at the Great American Beer Festival. This is a title that we are very, very proud of. We beat out our good friends at Figueroa Mountain Brewing Co. and Noble Aleworks. ❋

THE BREWHOUSE

229 W. Montecito St., Santa Barbara, CA 93101
805-884-4664 • sbbrewhouse.com

Mon.-Fri. open at 11 am;
Sat. & Sun. open at 10 am

WHEN DID YOU OPEN?

1998.

WHAT ARE YOUR MOST POPULAR BEERS?

West Beach IPA.

WHICH BEERS ARE YOU PROUDEST OF?

Hard to single out a favorite beer because it's like asking a mother which of her children she likes the best.

HAVE YOUR BEERS WON ANY AWARDS?

Yes. We used to enter the Cal. Craft Beer Competition at the Cal. State Fair, where we won a total of 21 first, second, or third place awards between 2004 and 2011, including first runner-up for best beer in the state in 2009 for our Bonnie Jean Scotch Ale. We quit entering because we ran out of room to display ribbons.

WHAT ARE THE BIGGEST CHALLENGES YOUR BREWERY HAS FACED?

We had a fire in the back bar that forced us to close for four months. But it was a chance to give the place, which had been open for almost 20 years, a face-lift. When we reopened, the regulars flocked back.

WHAT'S THE ATMOSPHERE LIKE?

Relaxed, laid-back. People say it has the feel of old-time Santa Barbara. One of my favorite reviews called us "Citronelle in a garage" (Citronelle was a local four-star restaurant). We're not much to look at, but the food is first rate.

ARE YOU DOG & FAMILY FRIENDLY?

Yes, we have a dog-friendly patio and even a doggie menu.

DO YOU HAVE FOOD?

We're a brewpub, with a full menu ranging from basic pub fare (burgers, fish and chips) to steaks, pasta, and seafood. Our most popular dish is the filet mignon enchiladas.

Our motto is "You don't have to be a rocket scientist, but it helps," because our head brewer used to be a rocket scientist who worked for NASA in Houston in the space shuttle guidance system. He discovered craft beers in the late eighties, but Santa Barbara didn't have one, so he started homebrewing, which became a passion, and a couple of years later he opened the brewery, which doubled the number of breweries in SB at the time.

The brewery's three owners get along great because they each have their own focus: one's the brewer, one's the chef, and one books the bands for the live music shows.

Every October, we make a big deal of Oktoberfest. We set up long tables out back, the servers dress in lederhosen or dirndls, there is a 12-piece tuba band, we serve brats and sauerbraten, and we generally turn the place into a German beer hall.

Santa Barbara is home to a very friendly, collaborative craft brewing scene, sharing or trading equipment and helping each other out at tough times, such as when we had the fire. ✻

CAPTAIN FATTY'S

6483 Calle Real, Unit D, Goleta, CA 93117
captainfattys.com

Mon.-Fri. 3:30-9 pm;
Sat. noon-10 pm; Sun. noon-8 pm

WHEN DID YOU OPEN?
November 2014. The company was alive and making beer in 2013 but didn't open a tasting room till 2014.

WHAT ARE YOUR MOST POPULAR BEERS?
Calypso Cucumber Sour; The Blue IPA.

WHICH BEERS ARE YOU PROUDEST OF?
We are most proud of the Calypso Cucumber Sour. Sour beer fanatics enjoy it, as do people who don't love or haven't tried sour beers before.

HAVE YOUR BEERS WON ANY AWARDS?
We won a gold medal for Kalliope, in the Berliner Weisse category at GABF 2017.

WHAT'S THE ATMOSPHERE LIKE?
It's a very mellow vibe. We love to make new beers, keep the menu diverse, and see the customer reaction to trying our new beers.

ARE YOU DOG & FAMILY FRIENDLY?
Yes, we are both dog and kid friendly. ✳

80

M.SPECIAL BREWING CO.

6860 Cortona Dr., Suite C, Goleta, CA 93117
805-968-6500 • mspecialbrewco.com

Sun.–Thurs. 11:30 am–9 pm;
Fr. & Sat. 11:30–10 pm

WHEN DID YOU OPEN?
September 2015.

WHAT ARE YOUR MOST POPULAR BEERS?
M.Special American Lager; Greatland IPA; Dozer American Brown Ale.

HAVE YOUR BEERS WON ANY AWARDS?
Lazy Eye DIPA: silver, SD International Beer Fest; Dozer Brown Ale: silver, SD International Beer Fest.

WHAT'S THE ATMOSPHERE LIKE?
Good beer, every time.

ARE YOU DOG & FAMILY FRIENDLY?
Yes and yes.

DO YOU HAVE FOOD?
Food trucks.

WHAT ELSE CAN YOU TELL US?
We're a music hub, and for such a small place, we've had some big visitors.

Our American Lager is a throwback to a true American lager, only brewed fresh and local. ❋

HOLLISTER BREWING CO.

96980 Marketplace Dr., Goleta, CA 93117
805-968-2810 • hollisterbrewco.com

Tues.-Sat. 11 am-10 pm;
Sun. & Mon. 11 am-9 pm

WHEN DID YOU OPEN?

May 2007.

WHAT ARE YOUR MOST POPULAR BEERS?

The Pope IPA, Hippie Kicker IPA, Beachside Blonde.

WHICH BEERS ARE YOU PROUDEST OF?

Tiny Bubbles, The Pope IPA.

HAVE YOUR BEERS WON ANY AWARDS?

Yes. Hip Hop DIPA, Southern Chaos, and Tiny Bubbles all won awards, but we stopped entering contests in 2013 because we realized that we wanted to focus on making great beer our customers appreciated, not beer that fit into a category.

WHAT ARE THE BIGGEST CHALLENGES YOUR BREWERY HAS FACED?

Educating the customer on all the different styles of beers we

make. We have anywhere from 15 to 17 beers on tap that we brew on-site. Everyone wants IPA, and we have three to six different IPA styles on at all times, but there are other really great beers on tap that can go underappreciated.

WHAT'S THE ATMOSPHERE LIKE?
We have several different atmospheres going at once; a TV-free patio, an intimate bar, and a dining room with TVs. We are not a sports bar, but we do have TVs for people to enjoy if they want. Phrases customers have used to describe us: "family friendly," "something for everyone," "innovative, fresh menu," "too many beers to just visit once!"

ARE YOU DOG & FAMILY FRIENDLY?
Yes, both!

DO YOU HAVE FOOD?
Yes, we make everything from scratch, from our ranch dressing to beer-battered fried pickles, fish tacos, chicken pot pie, and fresh pizzas.

WHAT ELSE CAN YOU TELL US?
Family owned and run. ✸

82

BANG THE DRUM

950 Orcutt Rd., San Luis Obispo, CA 93401
805-242-8372 • bangthedrumbrewery.com

Mon.-Thurs. 2-10 pm; Fri. & Sat. noon-midnight;
Sun. noon-10 pm

WHEN DID YOU OPEN?

Our tasting room opened in August 2013; however, we were brewing before then.

WHAT ARE YOUR MOST POPULAR BEERS?

Our flagship Yerba Mate IPA is one of our top brews; our seasonal Strawberry Surprise Me and Maple Brown are also popular. Anything with a good balance of hops is always a hit, and we have regulars who call in to see if our Gluten Free IPA (I know, gluten free! Made with sorghum and honey) is on tap. All. Of. The. Time.

WHICH BEERS ARE YOU PROUDEST OF?

Because our beer turnover is so fast, we struggle to have a favorite. What we love is the fact we get to have such fresh beer, using local ingredients.

WHAT ARE THE BIGGEST CHALLENGES YOUR BREWERY HAS FACED?

Working with a three-BBL system is fun because we get to experiment with creative beers. However, it is difficult because we constantly have to brew to keep up with demand. We are working on growing our system in the near future.

We are located a couple of miles outside of downtown, and although that is plus for many of our customers, we lack the foot traffic of the downtown area. We have helped drive traffic by creating events with amazing local and traveling live bands, open mic and trivia nights, charity events, and themed beat dance parties.

WHAT'S THE ATMOSPHERE LIKE?

Our brewery feels more like a coffee shop than a traditional brewery. One of the cofounders, who is also an architect, took advantage of a nearby reclaimed wood and materials yard to create a rustic and earthy feel. We have a cozy indoor tasting room and big sliding doors we open to our beautiful and winding outdoor patio on warm, sunny days. Good vibes and service that makes you feel like you are a part of the family are an important part of our culture here. Happy beer and happy people.

ARE YOU DOG & FAMILY FRIENDLY?

We absolutely love dogs here, and we even have a brew dog named Porter who grew up in our tasting room.

We also love that most of our daytime and early evening events are family friendly. As long as neither drinks the beer, we are 100 percent kid and dog friendly.

DO YOU HAVE FOOD?

We usually have food trucks four or five nights out of the week.

WHAT ELSE CAN YOU TELL US?

This brewery was created by a father and daughter! As a result, we treat everyone in the company like we are in a small family.

Our head brewer is the only female head brewer in the county, and we are a largely female operated brewery.

We do not have a TV anywhere in our brewery. Instead, we have drums and other rhythmic instruments for our patrons to play on and have live music events two to four times a week. ❋

83

MANROCK BREWING CO.

1750 El Camino Real, Suite A, Grover Beach, CA 93433
805-270-3089 • manrockbrewing.com

Mon. & Tues. 3–9 pm; Wed.–Sat. noon–10 pm;
Sun. noon–7 pm

WHEN DID YOU OPEN?
September 2012.

WHAT ARE YOUR MOST POPULAR BEERS?
Fear the Reaper Amber Ale; Sand Pail Pale Ale; Beach Town IPA; Bag O'Bones Brown; Night Cap Stout.

WHICH BEERS ARE YOU PROUDEST OF?
Amber, pale ale, IPA, and brown. Our beers are full flavored and crisp, with unique character.

HAVE YOUR BEERS WON ANY AWARDS?
Yes, our amber and our Follow the Crows IPA.

WHAT ARE THE BIGGEST CHALLENGES YOUR BREWERY HAS FACED?
Financing our equipment with our own money.

No investors, family owned and operated.

ARE YOU DOG & FAMILY FRIENDLY?
Patio is dog friendly and we are family friendly.

DO YOU HAVE FOOD?
Yes, handmade wood-fired pizza, handmade jumbo pretzels, nachos, loaded franks, fries.

WHAT ELSE CAN YOU TELL US?
ManRock is short for Mansfield Rock, which is our great grandparents' rock located off of the coast of Highway One. They homesteaded here in 1888! ❄

UNDERGROUND BREWING CO.

1040 Broad St., San Luis Obispo, CA 93401
805-439-4200 • undergroundbrewco.com

Wed.–Sat. noon–1 am;
Sun. noon–10 pm

WHEN DID YOU OPEN?
August 2016 (as Metro Brew).

WHAT ARE YOUR MOST POPULAR BEERS?
Limitless IPA and our kolsch.

WHICH BEERS ARE YOU PROUDEST OF?
Our beers are like children—
we love all of them equally.

HAVE YOUR BEERS WON ANY AWARDS?
They will. Just stay tuned.

WHAT ARE THE BIGGEST CHALLENGES YOUR BREWERY HAS FACED?
Location, location, location.

WHAT'S THE ATMOSPHERE LIKE?
We are inclusive, not exclusive.

ARE YOU DOG & FAMILY FRIENDLY?
Yes and yes, even invisible
friends.

DO YOU HAVE FOOD?
Pub grub, dogs, brats, pretzels,
wings.

WHAT ELSE CAN YOU TELL US?
As a business, we are totally
creative, compassionate, and truly
a craft brewery.

We have an entire chalk wall
for your creativity in our full bar.

The train printed in the taproom is just like the one on *Soul
Train*. ❄

FIRESTONE

1400 Ramada Dr., Paso Robles, CA 93446
805-225-5911 • www.FirestoneBeer.com

Daily 10 am–5 pm

WHEN DID YOU OPEN?
1996.

WHAT ARE YOUR MOST POPULAR BEERS?
DBA, Union Jack, Luponic Distortion, and 805.

WHICH BEERS ARE YOU PROUDEST OF?
Each of our beers has a purpose and story behind it that we're

proud of. That'd be like choosing a favorite child!

HAVE YOUR BEERS WON ANY AWARDS?
Nearly all of our broad-market beers have won awards.

WHAT ARE THE BIGGEST CHALLENGES YOUR BREWERY HAS FACED?
We were brewing at max capacity for a few years, but now we

have a new brewhouse, so our brewers get their weekends back.

WHAT'S THE ATMOSPHERE LIKE?
We believe in "beer before glory" at Firestone Walker, and that is felt throughout the whole brewery. Nothing would be possible without making great beer first.

ARE YOU DOG & FAMILY FRIENDLY?
Definitely family friendly!

DO YOU HAVE FOOD?
We have a full restaurant with a range of food items that pair perfectly with our beers. Tacos, pizzas, burgers, and more.

WHAT ELSE CAN YOU TELL US?
We also have a taproom and blending center in Buellton and an experimental brewery in Venice.

The dueling Lion and Bear represent our cofounders, who are in constant battle with each other, but then always come together for the love of beer.

Brewmaster Matt Brynildson's nickname is "Merlin" because he is a wizard in the brewhouse. ❋

FIRESTONE WALKER®
BREWING COMPANY

Inland Empire

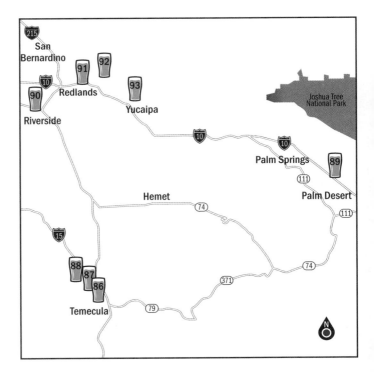

86. Aftershock Brewing Co., Temecula

87. Refuge Brewery, Temecula

88. Relentless Brewing Co., Temecula

89. La Quinta Brewing Co., Palm Desert

90. Euryale, Riverside

91. Escape Craft Brewery, Redlands

92. Hangar 24, Redlands

93. Brewcaipa Brewing Co., Yucaipa

86

AFTERSHOCK

28822 Old Town Front St., #108, Temecula, CA 92590
951-972-2256 • aftershockbrewing.com

Mon. & Tues. 3–8 pm;
Wed.–Sat. 1–10 pm; Sun. 1–8 pm

WHEN DID YOU OPEN?
September 2012.

WHAT ARE YOUR MOST POPULAR BEERS?
Orange CreamsicAle, Oatmeal Raisin Cookie Ale (ORCA), Peanut Alert.

WHICH BEERS ARE YOU PROUDEST OF?
Oatmeal Raisin Cookie Ale—we've been able to combine two different things (beer and cookies) and make it work. And win awards for it. Ha!

HAVE YOUR BEERS WON ANY AWARDS?
Oatmeal Raisin Cookie Ale, Richter Rauch (smoked ale).

WHAT ARE THE BIGGEST CHALLENGES YOUR BREWERY HAS FACED?
Manageable growth. Distributors breaking contracts.

WHAT'S THE ATMOSPHERE LIKE?
Cozy. People have described us as "unique" and "pushing the limits of what beer can be."

DO YOU HAVE FOOD?
No, just bar snacks. Jerky, nuts, popcorn, etc. ❄

REFUGE BREWERY

43040 Rancho Way, Temecula, CA 92590
951-506-0609 • refugebrew.com

Tues.–Thurs. open at 3:00 pm;
Fri.–Sun. open at noon

WHEN DID YOU OPEN?
December 2012.

WHAT ARE YOUR MOST POPULAR BEERS?
Blood Orange Wit.

WHICH BEERS ARE YOU PROUDEST OF?
We do a lot of incurable barrel-aged Belgian-style beers.

HAVE YOUR BEERS WON ANY AWARDS?
Blood Orange Wit won gold at the 2017 GABF for fruited Belgian-style beers.

WHAT ARE THE BIGGEST CHALLENGES YOUR BREWERY HAS FACED?
Distribution out of our home market.

WHAT'S THE ATMOSPHERE LIKE?
Cozy and educational, lots of visibility on the brewing process.

ARE YOU DOG & FAMILY FRIENDLY?
Patio for dogs, and, yes, family friendly.

DO YOU HAVE FOOD?
No, but we often have food trucks.

WHAT ELSE CAN YOU TELL US?
We are the largest brewery in Riverside County.

One day a customer randomly brought in blood oranges and it led to our best-selling beer. ❊

RELENTLESS BREWING CO.

42030 Avenida Alvarado, Suite F, Temecula, CA 92590
951-296-9400 • relentlessbrewing.com
Wed.–Fri. 3–8 pm;
Sat. 1–9 pm; Sun. 1–6 pm

WHEN DID YOU OPEN?
January 2016.

WHAT ARE YOUR MOST POPULAR BEERS?
IPAs and stouts.

WHICH BEERS ARE YOU PROUDEST OF?
Sours, because they are original

and we try to barrel-age them not only in wine barrels but in other barrels, such as tequila and whiskey.

HAVE YOUR BEERS WON ANY AWARDS?
Yes. San Diego Beer Festival for our IPA The Bear, the Witch, and the Ice Axe. We won silver.

WHAT ARE THE BIGGEST CHALLENGES YOUR BREWERY HAS FACED?

Being in a town that has not embraced sours yet.

WHAT'S THE ATMOSPHERE LIKE?

Casual, easy going. Good sours take time. Great sours take patience.

ARE YOU DOG & FAMILY FRIENDLY?

Yes to both.

DO YOU HAVE FOOD?

No, but we have food trucks occasionally.

WHAT ELSE CAN YOU TELL US?

Vinnie Cilurzo, the owner of Russian River, is from Temecula. He was the brewer and owner of a brewery called The Blind Pig. They were located on Avenida Alvarado, which closed down many years ago. Our brewery is currently on that same street.

When you come in, you will feel like it was definitely not made by a contractor. My husband and I did everything ourselves with the help of our close friends.

All the wood that was torn down was used to make the bar. The pallets we get from grain are used to hang our merchandise. Our cold room was such an eyesore, our friend came in and spray-painted graffiti art all over it. Our walls were also ugly, so we had local artists and vendors display their artwork. You gotta come check it out. We love art and supporting local artists. ✽

LA QUINTA BREWING CO.

Brewery: 77917 Wildcat Dr., Palm Desert, CA 92211
760-200-2597 • laquintabrewing.com

Daily 2–8 pm

Old Town Taproom: 78-065 Main St. #100, La Quinta, CA 92211
760-972-4251 • laquintabrewing.com

Sun.-Thurs. noon–10 pm; Fri. & Sat. noon–midnight

WHEN DID YOU OPEN?
November 2013.

WHAT ARE YOUR MOST POPULAR BEERS?
Even Par 7.2 IPA; Poolside Blonde.

WHICH BEERS ARE YOU PROUDEST OF?
Even Par 7.2 IPA—it's our best-selling beer.

HAVE YOUR BEERS WON ANY AWARDS?
Yes, nine in 2017. Bourbon barrel–aged Koffi Porter won the 2016 World Cup gold.

WHAT ARE THE BIGGEST CHALLENGES YOUR BREWERY HAS FACED?

Starting a brewery in an area that historically didn't have craft beer.

WHAT'S THE ATMOSPHERE LIKE?

Quaint, comfortable, cozy.

ARE YOU DOG & FAMILY FRIENDLY?

Yes and yes.

DO YOU HAVE FOOD?

No food.

WHAT ELSE CAN YOU TELL US?

The brewery was founded by a local who started homebrewing less than two years prior to opening the brewery after he received a "Mr. Beer" homebrewing kit from his wife for Christmas.

Our current brewer, Skip Madsen, started brewing at the Pike Brewing Company more than 25 years ago.

Our brewery is one of only two production breweries in the Coachella Valley (the greater Palm Springs area). Both opened in 2013 within three months of each other. ❖

90

EURYALE

2060 Chicago Ave., #A-17, Riverside, CA 92507
951-530-8865 • euryalebrewing.com

Wed.–Sat. noon–10 pm

WHEN DID YOU OPEN?
April 2016.

WHAT ARE YOUR MOST POPULAR BEERS?
Iota IPA, Cyclopes Coconut Porter, Euryale ESB.

WHICH BEERS ARE YOU PROUDEST OF?
We are proud of all of our beers. Brewmaster Don puts passion into every one of them. Our beers are very drinkable and we strive to make our beer—eurale (the Y is silent because the beer speaks for itself).

HAVE YOUR BEERS WON ANY AWARDS?
Not yet.

WHAT ARE THE BIGGEST CHALLENGES YOUR BREWERY HAS FACED?
The time it took to get open (city permits especially), getting the word out to the community, and other business problems that face any start-up/family business—"time and money."

WHAT'S THE ATMOSPHERE LIKE?
A place where you can kick back, play games, hang out, and drink great beer. Patrons routinely say, "I didn't know you were here; we'll be back" and "Cyclopes Coconut Porter, pure heaven."

ARE YOU DOG & FAMILY FRIENDLY?
Family friendly.

DO YOU HAVE FOOD?
Not really; we have complimentary pretzels and sell locally made beef jerky.

WHAT ELSE CAN YOU TELL US?
The Euryale ESB is Carrie's birthday beer. When Euryale first opened, Carrie asked Don to make an ESB. This was a style of beer that Don had introduced her to when they visited Widmer Bros. Brewery in Portland, Oregon. She asked him to suggest a beer from the menu that she might like; she was just starting the journey of discov-

ering she liked craft beer. He said, "Try the ESB." Carrie said, "ESB? What does that mean?" Don replied, "extra special bitter." Carrie complained, "I don't want a bitter beer." Don said, "Trust me, it's not bitter and you will like it." Well, Carrie loved the ESB; it was malty, slightly sweet, and caramel-y. Carrie thought an ESB would be a great addition to Euryale's taps. Don was reluctant; he said, "I have beers in mind that I want to make; I'm planning to do this and that." Well, a few months later, at the beginning of March (Carrie's birthday is March 4th),

Don asked Carrie, "What do you want for your birthday?" Carrie replied, "I want you to make an ESB." Don made a delicious ESB; it was one of the seasonal beers, and it was so popular it was on tap for six-plus months. We have only six taps, so we eventually had to rotate some new beers in, and the ESB left the tap. We got many requests for that beer, and now Carrie and the Euryale ESB fans are happy to have it back. Carrie loves introducing people to this English-style pale ale. If they ask what ESB means, she says "extra special beer, you gotta try it." ❋

RIVERSIDE   CALIFORNIA

ESCAPE CRAFT BREWERY

721 Nevada St., #401, Redlands, CA 92373
909-713-3727 • EscapeCraftBrewery.com
Tues.-Sat. noon-9:30 pm;
Sun. noon-8 pm

WHEN DID YOU OPEN?
January 2015.

WHAT ARE YOUR MOST POPULAR BEERS?
Sakura, a cherry blossom white wheat made with cherry blossom green tea; Redlands Nights, an orange blossom blonde ale celebrating our citrus heritage; Lazy Day IPA, smooth and clean with citrus-noted hops (Mosaic and Centennial); Midnight Express, house-roasted Thai coffee infused with cocoa into our oatmeal milk stout—my breakfast beer of choice!

WHICH BEERS ARE YOU PROUDEST OF?
For a unique, crowd-pleasing favorite, Sakura is amazing. Crisp and full flavored, it uncommonly appeals to both mild, mellow drinkers as well as hopheads, maybe because of its

superclean finish and refreshing snap. Falling Up IPL was our second anniversary brew, and it didn't disappoint—tons of Citra and Galaxy hops provided bright hop-forward notes of pineapple, citrus, and mango and a super clean finish.

HAVE YOUR BEERS WON ANY AWARDS?
Yes: "B.E.E.R.S." festival in LA Best of Show; 2017 Cal. State Fair Commercial Craft Beer Competition.

WHAT ARE THE BIGGEST CHALLENGES YOUR BREWERY HAS FACED?
Keeping up with production demand while continuing to create fun seasonals can be a little crazy; but so many of the fun ones become favorites! Being husband-and-wife owned and operated, we take care of opposite ends of the business, so we're both always busy and in

the mix, and we often set up and run the numerous events Escape is invited to pour at, so weekends off are rare!

WHAT'S THE ATMOSPHERE LIKE?

Our space is very casual and pretty funky. We have an old travel theme, with lots of vintage steamer trunks and furniture made out of car parts, bicycle sprockets, motorcycles, a wing from an experiential airplane. Our tables are made with doors from a historical hotel in our city that was torn down in the seventies. Old suitcases are everywhere, including our menu board because a suitcase means you are about to go on an adventure = escape from ordinary beer.

Our fav motto is "We travel not to escape life but for life not to escape us."

DO YOU HAVE FOOD?

We have a great Mexican food truck every Wednesday.

WHAT ELSE CAN YOU TELL US?

Josh is the head brewer/owner; he was a professional firefighter/ paramedic. We have a great time naming our beers, which are usually based on funny movie lines and travel. The majority of our beers are "gluten reduced" to fall within the U.S. and European gluten-free requirements, but we don't really advertise it, it's like an insider's secret . . . they taste totally normal. ❁

HANGAR 24

1710 Sessums Dr., Redlands, CA 92374
909-389-1400 • hangar24brewery.com

Sun.–Thurs. 11 am–10 pm;
Sat. & Sun. 11 am–11 pm

WHEN DID YOU OPEN?
2008.

WHAT ARE YOUR MOST POPULAR BEERS?
Orange Wheat, 24 Blonde Ale, and Betty IPA are the best-selling offerings. Pugachev's Cobra, a barrel-aged Russian imperial stout, is released annually in early winter and has an intense and loyal following.

WHICH BEERS ARE YOU PROUDEST OF?
Orange Wheat is not only our most popular offering, we are proud to say it includes whole oranges grown minutes from the production brewery and never contains any artificial flavoring. Betty IPA was born from our quest to deliver not only a fresh hoppy offering that would have long-lasting appeal, but one that would define its own category in the genre, which we feel it has. And our Pugachev's Cobra, from our acclaimed Barrel Roll series, has vaulted to the head of the class when it comes to bourbon barrel–aged stouts, while the variant Pugachev's Royale has become a highly lauded and sought-after delicacy.

HAVE YOUR BEERS WON ANY AWARDS?
From gold at the GABF to an array of hardware earned at a number of local and regional competitions, we have been humbled to receive copious amounts of validation from peers in the industry. But because beer is a personal experience, we'll leave judgment to each individual as to which full glass of chilled H24 beer fits them best.

WHAT ARE THE BIGGEST CHALLENGES YOUR BREWERY HAS FACED?
The changing landscape of the brewing industry has provided many challenges to outfits both large and small, Hangar 24 in-

cluded. The brewery had the fortune of opening in 2008, before the height of the craft beer boom. There were changes aplenty in those early days, both in-house and within the industry itself.

With more than 6,000 U.S. breweries in operation as of 2017, consumers have options like never before, with more and more great beer at their reach. Positioning yourself in that crowded landscape has its own quirks. Ultimately, though, it comes down to a couple simple tenets: Brew quality beer with unsurpassed consistency, and listen when the customer speaks.

What's the atmosphere like?

A welcoming atmosphere with a dedication to customer service, along with plenty of open-air seating and amazing views of the nearby San Bernardino Mountains, as well as operations at the Redlands Municipal Airport across the street. Hangar 24 has developed into a community gathering place. That community has provided unwavering support from the beginning, and the brewery would not be where it is without a loyalty that we feel has pulled us into the fabric of the local scene.

Are you dog & family friendly?

Dogs are welcome and the brewery is family friendly.

Do you have food?

Food is not served. Food trucks are on the premises on occasion. Outside food is welcome, and food deliveries from nearby restaurants can be made.

What else can you tell us?

Hangar 24's main brewery building was built during World War II at the former Norton Air Force Base and eventually moved 9 miles to its present location in Redlands. The building was used to manufacture biplanes, operate a flight school, provide book storage, and for a religious outreach program before Hangar 24 set up operation in 2008.

Owner/brewmaster Ben Cook was a homebrewer and received his pilot's license before opening Hangar 24. He has since used his vision to turn his former hobbies into a regional brewery and has started two annual air shows: AirFest in Redlands, California, in late spring and AirFest in Lake Havasu City, Arizona, in the fall. ❖

BREWCAIPA BREWING CO.

35058 Yucaipa Blvd., Yucaipa, CA 92399
909-797-2337 • brewcaipa.com

Wed. & Thurs. 2-10 pm; Fri. & Sat. noon-midnight;
Sun: noon-8 pm

WHEN DID YOU OPEN?
March 2017.

WHAT ARE YOUR MOST POPULAR BEERS?
Blonde #1—taste: honey, crisp, biscuit-y; Brewcaipa #2—taste: West Coast smooth, sessionable IPA.

WHICH BEERS ARE YOU PROUDEST OF?
We are proudest of our double IPA, Wild Parody, due to the exotic variety of hops, high ABV, and sessionability.

HAVE YOUR BEERS WON ANY AWARDS?
We have not entered our beer into any contests, *yet.*

WHAT ARE THE BIGGEST CHALLENGES YOUR BREWERY HAS FACED?
We are brewing mostly Old World–style ales and lagers in a town that doesn't know much about craft beer. Educating our

consumers on the different kinds of beers and flavors that accompany a delicious craft brew is a bit of a challenge.

What's the atmosphere like?

We are part of a small town where we want everyone to feel like family. When you enter, we welcome you in, and when you leave, we say, "See ya tomorrow!" Our beer-tenders are trained to meet your personal tastes and learn your name for next time. We are very patriotic and support the amazing country we live in.

Are you dog & family friendly?

We are both dog and family friendly. Dogs are allowed on and near the patio, and we provide several nonalcoholic home-made sodas on tap for those who do not or cannot drink.

Do you have food?

We offer a variety of prepack-aged jerky and chips, or you can bring in food from a vendor of your choice! We also carry menus from several nearby food establishments that regularly deliver here.

What else can you tell us?

Scott, the owner, built this place with just a dream and his two hands. He is a visionary and unstoppable, a retired fire chief from Loma Linda Fire, and he almost lost his life on a call. He was on the fire engine's ladder when the driver accidentally hit a power line. The doctors couldn't believe he was still alive, but he fought back and eventually opened his dream brewery, Brewcaipa. To this day, he focuses on the development of the little town of Yucaipa and celebrating those protecting and defending our country and safety. An American flag is on every employee's shirt on the arm, and a giant wooden American flag hangs above the entrance. ❋

Imperial and Kern Counties

Imperial

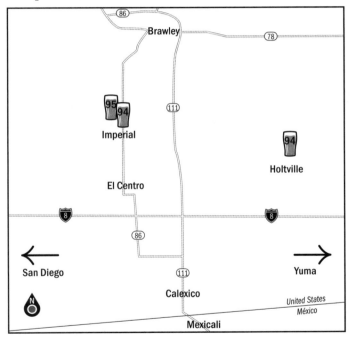

Kern

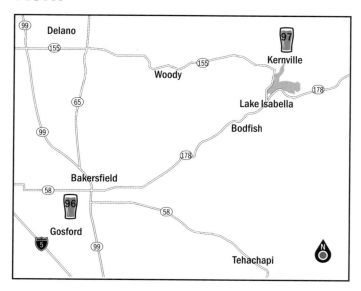

96. Lengthwise Brewing Co., Bakersfield
97. Kern River Brewing Co., Kernville

HUMBLE FARMER BREWING CO.

Brewery: 438 Walnut Ave., Holtville, CA 92250
760-356-7066 • humblefarmerbrewing.com

Thurs.–Sat. 3 pm–9 pm

Brewpub: 116 South Imperial Ave., Suite C, Imperial, CA 92251
760-356-7066 • www.humblefarmerbrewing.com

Mon.-Thurs. 3–10 pm; Fri. 3 pm–midnight;
Sat. 11 am–midnight; Sun. open at 10 am

WHEN DID YOU OPEN?
March 2016.

WHAT ARE YOUR MOST POPULAR BEERS?
Bordertown Blonde has been our best seller since day one. It's a nice, light beer made with local honey, and goes down easy in our hot climate. 80 Acre Carrot Ale, Highline Stout, and our IPAs have also been steady favorites in the community.

WHICH BEERS ARE YOU PROUDEST OF?
We're very proud of our beers that use local ingredients from the Imperial Valley's ag industry. That would be our 80 acre Carrot Ale, Bordertown Blonde, Alamo Rio Hazy IPA, Valley Summer

Lager, and many more. We use honey, lemons, melons, grapefruit, and durum wheat all grown and harvested within a few miles of the brewery. It's something that sets us apart from the many breweries out there today, and we believe fresh products contribute to great beer production.

HAVE ANY OF YOUR BEERS WON AWARDS?
Our 80 Acre Carrot Ale won a silver medal at the Great American Beer Festival this year, and we were extremely surprised and excited about it—we never expected to win an award when we set out to make a beer using carrots.

WHAT ARE THE BIGGEST CHALLENGES YOUR BREWERY HAS FACED?

Our valley's heat is definitely the biggest challenge during the summer. We're up around 115–120°F for a couple months of the summer, and it wreaks havoc on our chilling system and makes brew days extremely hot in the brew room.

WHAT'S THE ATMOSPHERE LIKE?

We have a very casual and fun atmosphere. We host monthly cornhole tournaments, support the local music scene, and host regular events to keep things fun. One customer said, "Every desert needs a great watering hole, and Humble Farmer is that."

ARE YOU DOG & FAMILY FRIENDLY?

Yes to both!

DO YOU HAVE FOOD?

Yes, we have a full menu at our Imperial location. It is mostly good, old-fashioned pub food, and whatever is currently harvested in the valley.

WHAT ELSE CAN YOU TELL US?

We were the first brewery to open in the Imperial Valley.

We're always pushing the envelope when trying to add local products to our beer. Many times it turns out to be a bad idea (brewing with alfalfa or desert flora) and doesn't make it into commercial batches, but it definitely keeps things fun and interesting.

"Work hard, stay humble." ❄

PENTAGONAL BREWING CO.

115 N. Imperial Ave., Suite A, Imperial, CA 92251
760-545-1045 • pentagonalbrewingcompany

Mon. 4–9 pm; Wed.–Fri. 3 pm–midnight;
Sat. 2 pm–midnight; Sun. 2–9 pm

WHEN DID YOU OPEN?

February 2017

WHAT ARE YOUR MOST POPULAR BEERS?

Lineman's Lager is the fan favorite. Light, easy drinking, and full of flavor. Parallel Universe, our double IPA, has quickly become the go-to for many of our patrons—an aggressively hopped DIPA with fruity notes and intense hoppy aromas.

WHICH BEERS ARE YOU PROUDEST OF?

Going against what one normally would do, antistainless Funke Monkey is a Belgian-style wild ale, fermented in an open red wine barrel with cherries added. We allowed this beer to age for six months before kegging it, and it was beyond worth it. Complex, tart, and with just the right amount of sweetness, Funke Monkey was a creation that we were nervous about. The uncertainties of open fermenta-

tion and a beer that we had not tried before turned out to be very tasty. Incredibly fun beer to make, it's what craft beer is all about: taking interesting ingredients and marrying them together in a glorious fermentation.

HAVE YOUR BEERS WON ANY AWARDS?
We haven't entered any contests.

WHAT ARE THE BIGGEST CHALLENGES YOUR BREWERY HAS FACED?
Changing a culture. The Imperial Valley has long been served solely by macrobeer. When we opened, there was only one other brewery, and that was mainly serving one portion of the greater Imperial Valley. As such, we were met with a lot of "do you have Bud/Coors/Miller Lite?" It is still a work in progress, but we have opened many people's eyes to the flavors independent craft beer can provide. Lineman's Lager, Ohana Pilsner, and our Red Tractor Ale are all favorites of those who are new to the world of craft beer.

WHAT'S THE ATMOSPHERE LIKE?
We offer a family-friendly, laid-back environment that all can enjoy. Company parties, personal celebrations, a night out, live music, arts and crafts, and relaxation are things you can find on a weekly basis at Pentagonal. Painting classes, live music, adoption events with the Imperial Valley Humane Society, cupcake pairings with Alba's Cake Studio, bike nights, comedy shows, open mic nights, and weekly trivia nights are what make Pentagonal Brewing Company the only place to offer something for everyone in the Imperial Valley.

ARE YOU DOG & FAMILY FRIENDLY?
Yes and yes.

DO YOU SERVE FOOD?
No food. Food trucks when available.

WHAT ELSE CAN YOU TELL US?
"Pentagonal" is a mathematical theorem that states, in part, that when one side of a pentagon gets bigger, all sides have to get bigger to keep the same shape. We are four owners with amazing wives who make up our fifth member.

Our location used to be a Video 2000 movie rental store. There is still a VHS drop-off slot in one of our doors. A true piece of history!

We are located under the clock tower in Imperial, the center of downtown!

Dogs, pigs, chickens, and kittens have all paid us a visit.

Phrases customers have used to describe the brewery: "The go-to spot for entertainment for fun"; "Great beer, great people"; "Finally, a place for everyone!" ❋ 195

LENGTHWISE BREWING CO.

7700 District Blvd., Bakersfield, CA 93313
661-836-2537 • lengthwise.com

Mon.-Thurs. 11 am–10 pm;
Fri.-Sun. 11 am–7 pm

WHEN DID YOU OPEN?
First opened in July 1998; new location in June 2016.

WHAT ARE YOUR MOST POPULAR BEERS?
Zeus Imperial IPA.

WHICH BEERS ARE YOU PROUDEST OF?
Currently, our BBL-aged Saison aged in wine barrels for 12 months!

HAVE YOUR BEERS WON ANY AWARDS?
One. Centennial Ale silver

medal, World Beer Cup 2006.

WHAT ARE THE BIGGEST CHALLENGES YOUR BREWERY HAS FACED?

Adjusting to the size of the new location.

WHAT'S THE ATMOSPHERE LIKE?

Family atmosphere; the patio has Ping-Pong and cornhole. "Live life Lengthwise."

ARE YOU DOG & FAMILY FRIENDLY?

Sorry, no pets; bring your kids, as we feature a kids' menu.

DO YOU HAVE FOOD?

Pub-style food—burgers, sandwiches, salads; best known for our stinky fries! We also bake our bread fresh daily and feature our own spices, and the house coffee is roasted on-site.

WHAT ELSE CAN YOU TELL US?

Lengthwise means Live Experiences Now Great Things Happen When Inspiration Silences Excuses!!! ❁

KERN RIVER BREWING CO.

13415 Sierra Way, Kernville, CA 93238
760-376-2337 • kernriverbrewing.com

Winter: Sun.-Thurs. 11 am–9 pm; Fri. & Sat. 11 am–9:30 pm (pub);
Fri. & Sat. 11 am–8 pm; Sun. 11 am–4 pm (backyard)

Summer: Sun.-Thurs. 11 am–9:30 pm; Fri. & Sat. 11 am–10 pm (pub);
Sun–Thurs. 11 am–8 pm; Fri. & Sat. 11 am–9 pm (backyard)

WHEN DID YOU OPEN?

2006.

WHAT ARE YOUR MOST POPULAR BEERS?

We are most known for our IPAs, especially Citra Double IPA. Our four flagship beers—Just Outstanding IPA, Isabella Blonde, Sequoia Red, and Class V Stout—have remained popular over the last 12 years. Most recently, Chuuurch! West Coast IPA has become something we are very proud of, and we're working hard to keep up with its demand around California.

WHICH BEERS ARE YOU PROUDEST OF?

Citra DIPA definitely put us on the map.

HAVE YOUR BEERS WON ANY AWARDS?

Yes! Most notably, Citra DIPA took gold in the 2011 GABF.

WHAT ARE THE BIGGEST CHALLENGES YOUR BREWERY HAS FACED?

We love our small town, but you have to learn to rise and fall with the tourism seasons, drought, and turnover in staff.

WHAT'S THE ATMOSPHERE LIKE?

We are definitely a small community where "everybody knows your name." Since we have two restaurants on one property, we have a little something for everyone. Want a small-town pub with tasty burgers? Go to the pub! Want a braised beef flatbread with a view of the mountains and a shiny production brewery? Go to the backyard!

ARE YOU DOG & FAMILY FRIENDLY?

Yes, the patios at both locations are dog friendly to friendly leashed dogs. Children are welcome!

DO YOU HAVE FOOD?

Our pub is your local burger joint with waffle fries and the ever-so-popular fried pickles! Our newest addition, the backyard, which has no fryer, offers up creamy mac 'n cheese, sandwiches, and several delicious options on your choice of flatbread, smashed potatoes, or roasted butternut squash.

WHAT ELSE CAN YOU TELL US?

KRBC owners Eric and Rebecca Giddens found the Kern River because of their love of kayaking. Both spent time on the U.S. Olympic team, and Rebecca won a silver medal in the 2004 Olympic Games in Athens in the Women's K-1 slalom competition.

Our director of brewery operations, Shaun Morgan, got his brewing start with Pizza Port–Bressi Ranch in San Diego. ❋

Alphabetical List of Breweries

Cheers

Nigel Quinney lives in San Diego County, where he drinks a lot of excellent beer. Deirdre Greene lives in the Bay Area, where she drinks a lot of equally excellent beer. When they are not drinking beer—and sometimes even when they are—they run Roaring Forties Press, a publishing company that focuses on travel, the arts, popular culture, and contemporary issues.

Nigel and Deirdre have many people to thank for their invaluable support and help during the making of this book. Wesley Palmer deserves all the thanks we can give him for his various and substantial contributions—indeed, Wes should probably be considered a third author for his tireless research, unflagging enthusiasm, inventive ideas, and ability to charm even the grumpiest of brewers! Dennis Williams, one of the owners of Culture Brewing Co., provided extremely helpful suggestions early in the research for this book.

Our design and production team was outstanding. Kim Rusch came up with the perfect covers. Karen Weldon laid out the book with wonderful flair and professionalism; we don't know what we do without her. Kaileen Smith produced precise but unfussy maps—no small achievement! And Carla Castillo helped catch a small army of pesky typos.

Researching and producing a book like this takes a lot of time. Please don't get us wrong: we're not complaining about that, especially because a lot of that time was in breweries! (As Wes has often remarked, researching the craft beer industry is surely one of the best jobs around.) But we're grateful to our families, who also didn't complain about the time we spent putting this book together. Deirdre would like to thank John, Phoebe, Sophie, and Celia Greene. Nigel owes a very big thanks to Kim, Juliet, and Beckett.

This book could not, of course, have been produced without the help of the people it spotlights: the brewers, brewery owners, brewery staff, and everyone else who make California craft brewing the toast of the beer-loving nation. We are indebted to them for their readiness to answer our questions and unearth all sorts of photos and artwork. As this book makes clear, craft brewing demands buckets of skill, energy, and love, and we are very grateful that, despite all the other demands on their time, the brewers featured in this book were prepared to share their experiences, thoughts, and stories with us. ❋

Notes

Notes

Notes

Notes

Notes